THE REAL MEANING OF THE ZODIAC

D. James Kennedy, Ph. D.

Compiled and edited by Nancy Britt
from a series of sermons on the Zodiac
by Dr. D. James Kennedy.

tcrm Publishing
Ft. Lauderdale, FL

CONTENTS

PREFACE

The heavens declare the glory of God; and the firmament sheweth his handiwork. Day unto day uttereth speech, and night unto night sheweth knowledge. There is no speech nor language, where their voice is not heard. Their line is gone out through all the earth, and their words to the end of the world. In them hath he set a tabernacle for the sun, which is as a bridegroom coming out of his chamber, and rejoiceth as a strong man to run a race. His going forth is from the end of heaven, and his circuit unto the ends of it: and there is nothing hid from the heat thereof.

— Psalm 19:1-6

Have you ever taken an I.Q. test? If so, you probably came across questions that were expressed in this way: "A group of four things are set before you; three of them have something in common and one of them seems out of place. Find the one that does not belong". How about a little I.Q. test right now? In the first chapter of the Bible we read, **"And God said, Let there be lights in the firmament of the heaven to divide the day from the night; and let them be for signs, and for seasons, and for days, and years. . . . And God made two great lights; the greater light to rule the day, and the lesser light to rule the night: he made the stars also"** (Genesis 1:14,16).

Of the four things set before us in these verses, did not one of them seem strangely out of place? Some of you are saying: "What four?" Listen again: ". . . **and let them be for signs, and for seasons, and for days, and years.**" Does one of them seem out of place? It would be obvious to everyone with a modicum of knowledge of astronomy that the heavenly bodies have a great deal to say about our *years*, our *days* and our *seasons*. But how are they signs? What is a sign?

What Is A Sign?

A sign is something which proclaims a message. What is the message proclaimed by the stars? I would like to talk to you about what might be called "Biblical Astrology," or as I have titled it for our investigation: "The Gospel in the Stars."

There exists in the writings of virtually all civilized nations a description of the major stars in the heavens—something which might be called their "Constellations of the Zodiac" or the "Signs of the Zodiac," of which there are twelve. If you go back in time to Rome, or beyond that to Greece, or before that to Egypt, Persia, Assyria, or Babylonia—regardless of how far back you go, there is a remarkable phenomenon: Nearly all nations had the same twelve signs, representing the same twelve things, placed in the same order. Archaeologists, historians, and antiquarians have searched the dustiest libraries, uncovered the oldest tablets, ciphered the most difficult hieroglyphics, and have failed to discover how it is that in so many nations all over the world the same signs exist.

Remarkably, the stars in the heaven which represent those twelve signs bear absolutely no resemblance to the pictures of the signs themselves. For example, what we call the Big Dipper has been called Ursa Major (Great Bear). One thing it does not look like is a great bear. Neither do any of the other signs look like what they are supposed to represent.

Where Did They Come From?

Where did the signs come from? The book of Job, which is thought by many to be the oldest book in the Bible, goes back to approximately 2150 B.C., which is 650 years before Moses came upon the scene to write the Pentateuch; over 1,100 years before Homer wrote the *Odyssey* and the *Illiad*; and 1,500 years before Thales, the first of the philosophers, was born. In chapter 38, God finally breaks in and speaks to Job and to his false comforters. As He is questioning Job, showing him and his companions their ignorance, God says to them: **"Canst thou bind the sweet influences of Pleiades, or loose the bands of Orion? Canst thou bring forth Mazzaroth in his season? or canst thou guide Arcturus with his sons?"** (Job 38:31,32).

We see here reference to the constellations of Orion, Pleiades and Arcturus. Also in the book of Job there is reference to *Cetus, the Sea Monster*, and to *Draco, the Great Dragon*. I would call your attention to Job 38:32a: **"Canst thou bring forth Mazzaroth in his season?"** *Mazzaroth* is a Hebrew word which means "The Constellations of the Zodiac." In what may be the oldest book in all of human history, we find that the constellations of the zodiac were already clearly known and understood.

Where Did Their Names Come From?

The Bible tells us that God called all of the stars "the host of heaven"; that He numbered them, ordered them, and set them in the firmament to be signs. Their original meaning has been corrupted into something which was demonic, something which was satanic, something which was counterfeit, something which has given birth to what is known as modern astrology, and which the Bible repeatedly condemns and warns Christians against. It is a corruption which began at the Tower of Babel.

For example, in the book of Isaiah we read this admonition: "**Thou art wearied in the multitude of thy counsels. Let now the astrologers, the stargazers, the monthly prognosticators, stand up, and save thee from these things that shall come upon thee. Behold, they shall be as stubble; the fire shall burn them; they shall not deliver themselves from the power of the flame. . .**" **(Isaiah 47:13,14).** Even today many make their living by gazing at the stars to learn the future. They need to heed this warning from Isaiah. Jeanne Dixon and all of the rest should be warned they are in great danger. The Bible makes it very clear that these shall not be able to deliver even themselves from the power of the flame and they "**shall be as stubble,**" for they are heading for judgment and hellfire.

Having made it clear that the Bible expressly, explicitly, and repeatedly condemns what is now known as astrology, the fact remains that there was a God-given Gospel in the stars which lays beyond and behind that which has now been corrupted. I have studied numerous books on this subject, written by some great scholars, and would now like to bring to your attention some of their material.

We are told: "**The heavens declare the glory of God; and the firmament sheweth his handiwork. Day unto day uttereth speech, and night unto night sheweth knowledge. There is no speech nor language, where their voice is not heard**" **(Psalms 19:1-3).** God gave to all of the world a proclamation of the Gospel in the stars. It has been said a picture is worth a thousand words, and God has indeed painted the sky and made it a picture gallery replete with the glories of His redemption.

The first preaching of the Gospel is found in the third chapter of Genesis. Immediately after the temptation and fall of man, God made that first pronouncement when He said to Satan: **"And I will put enmity between thee and the woman, and between thy seed and her seed; it shall bruise thy head, and thou shalt bruise his heel" (Genesis 3:15).** It is called the *protoevangelium,* the first evangel, or first preaching of the Gospel. It says that God is going to put enmity between the serpent (Satan) and the woman, and between the seed of the serpent and the seed of the woman. Everywhere in the Scripture people are referred to as having come from a man. Only Christ is the seed of a woman, and the seed of the woman will **"bruise thy head, and thou shall bruise his heel."** This means that Satan was going to bruise the heel of Christ, bringing about His death on the cross. But He (Christ) would rise and totally and eternally destroy Satan. This is the first Gospel and this is what the pictures in the sky signify.

Satan's Lie

The distortion—the satanic counterfeit to this original proclamation of the Gospel is indeed tragic. Satan has always been and still is the great counterfeiter, the great deceiver who has deceived people into trusting in the sign rather than the thing God has signified.

For example: God created the Church to proclaim the Gospel. However, too many people trust in a church for their salvation. They want to find the "right" church, one which will save them. *No* church will save anyone. The Church points to Jesus Christ—the only Savior of man. Also, in the Lord's Supper, Christ gave to us the great tangible symbol of His death upon the cross. His broken body and shed blood point to the once-for-all atonement on the cross in which we should trust for our salvation. Instead, millions trust in the sacrament of the Lord's supper as their hope of salvation, rather than that which it signifies.

The Gospel in the stars is just another example of God's original message being perverted by Satan and sinful men. Instead of trusting in the Christ to which the stars point so gloriously, people who practice astrology trust in the stars themselves. The modern corruption of astrology expresses the idea that some mysterious, magical, and supernatural powers emanate from the houses of the zodiac, which affect and control destiny and lives. That is the lie of Satan which will destroy every soul that believes it. Instead, what God put in the stars is a glorious sky-painting of Jesus Christ as the Lord of Glory. Our goal is to rediscover this original message and proclaim it for God's glory.

The Zodiac and Christ

A hundred and some years ago, a skeptic by the name of Volney wrote a famous work entitled *Volney's Ruins*. He, along with Dupuis and Bailly and a number of French skeptics, gathered together a collection of all of the numerous ancient mythologies of the various peoples of the world, and demonstrated that these showed a remarkable and astounding correspondence to the teachings concerning Christ and His salvation.

They said that since these mythologies—which often involve interpretations of the constellations of the zodiac—very clearly long antedated the revelation and coming of Christ into the world, it was obvious to them that Christianity was nothing more than a borrowing from pagan mythology, dressed up in Hebrew dress and pawned off on a credulous world. Thus, many were led to a deeper examination of this concept and to some rather remarkable findings. One of the conclusions was the fact that none of the skeptics were able to tell whence came these ancient mythologies, and particularly this understanding of the signs of the zodiac—the constellations of the sky.

Where did these signs come from? These scholars discovered that their antiquity cannot be ascertained; no matter how far back we go, they are always still there! The earliest recorders of the signs describe something which happened prior to their day. This, by the way, can be determined because of something known as the "precession of the equinoxes." The fact that the stars change and shift in the sky over the centuries enables astronomers to know just when an event has taken place. Therefore, it is seen that from the very earliest days of mankind, these stars and signs have been known.

It is interesting that the signs bear little or no resemblance to the stars in the heavens. If a hundred people were to go out and name the constellations, they would not come up with the pictures that have been given to them and have been held by peoples all over the world.

According to Arabic tradition, the signs came from Seth and Enoch. This tradition is interesting since it links these signs to the grandson of Adam and says that Enoch and his father Seth (both men of faith) were the founders of this ancient understanding of the heavens.

Salvation Foretold

Therefore, from the very beginning, God has given a story of His salvation from which have come most of the ancient mythologies and ancient traditions. The signs are describing the salvation that would be wrought by Christ, and was given by God to Adam in the Garden of Eden. As mentioned before, this is called the *protoevangelium* (or the first evangel, the first Gospel), which was the very beginning of the revelation of Jesus Christ to the world, i.e., that the Seed of the woman would destroy the seed of the serpent.

Once again the efforts of the skeptics to try to make Christianity into something which is simply borrowed from paganism has failed.

This study answers questions about the text which states: **"For the invisible things of him from the creation of the world are clearly seen, being understood by the things that are made, even his eternal power and Godhead; so that they are without excuse" (Romans 1:20).** Further, **"So then faith cometh by hearing, and hearing by the word of God. But I say, Have they not heard? Yes verily, their sound went into all the earth, and their words unto the ends of the world." (Romans 10:17,18).** Their words (meaning their teaching, their instructions, their message) went into all of the world. That message is found in the star pictures, the art gallery of the heavens which God gave.

Job tells us: **"By his spirit he hath garnished [made bright or beautiful] the heavens; his hand hath formed the crooked [or fleeing] serpent" (Job 26:13).** One of the largest of the constellations in the skies is called **"The Crooked (or fleeing) Serpent."** Obviously God formed the stars into their particular positions; moreover, He also formed and gave the symbol or signification of it.

We are told in Genesis that God put the stars in the heavens for signs, and these signs convey a message. The theory we are presenting is that God revealed that message to Adam and to his sons and grandsons and that message has gone into all of the civilizations of the world and has been passed down through the centuries.

At the time of the building of the tower of Babel, this was corrupted into astrology. Thus, instead of these being signs of God and His salvation by which we should worship God, they were changed into deities, and people began to worship the sun, the moon, the planets, and the stars.

By the way, to the ancients, in addition to the sun and the moon, there were five planets visible to the naked eye, just as there are today: Mercury, Venus, Mars, Jupiter and Saturn. It is from those five planets and the sun and the moon that we get our names for the seven days of the week—all named after ancient pagan gods worshipped by pagan people.

It is well that you have nothing to do with modern astrology whatsoever because of its corruption and satanic aspects. But in order that you might appreciate what God has done, let us look briefly at the zodiac, its history and the birth of astrology.

Astrology Condemned

As we have seen, the Bible condemns astrology very strongly. Isaiah 47:13 states:

Thou art wearied in the multitude of thy counsels. Let now the astrologers, the stargazers, the monthly prognosticators, stand up, and save thee from these things that shall come upon thee. Behold, they shall be as stubble; the fire shall burn them; they shall not deliver themselves from the power of the flame: there shall not be a coal to warm at, nor fire to sit before it.

Instead of being simply the story of Christ, people took the heavenly signs to be deities which have an influence on our lives. Today this is covered over and now it is supposedly the stars themselves that are exerting some influence upon our lives. This is utterly absurd.

Astrologers try to justify this by saying that the moon influences the tides and it influences people's emotions, which is absolutely true. But the moon is 240,000 miles, or slightly less, away from the earth; whereas, stars are six thousand light-years and more away. (A light-year is over 5 1/2 trillion miles! That is over 35 quadrillion miles away—a figure so vast it is beyond our comprehension.) The stars do *not* exert any influence upon us and the deities they supposedly represent are but the figments of people's imaginations.

The Bible tells us we are not to consort with astrologers; we are not to consult them; we are not to have anything to do with astrology. And yet, originally, there was this great revelation of God, of His glory, and of His salvation in what has come to be known as the zodiac.

This is often described as a circle of animals. At a deep level we see the zodiac as *the* path, or *the* way, and it is *the* way of salvation revealed in the heavens. But that is not really what the word zodiac means. Rather, it comes from a primitive root, *zoad*, which comes from the Hebrew

14

sodi, and in Sanskrit means: "A Way," "A Path," "A Step."
At a deeper level we see the zodiac picturing The Path,
The Way of salvation revealed beautifully for us in the
heavens.

Affirmed in Secular Writings

It is interesting to see the history of this description
to mankind. Aratus, who lived from 400 to 350 B.C., wrote
a very famous work about the heavens called
Phaenomena, in which he described all of the
constellations and figures of the heavens. Interestingly,
Aratus was a native of Tarsus, as was the Apostle Paul.
His poem *Diosemeia* was the most famous and most
popular Greek poem next to the two famous poems of
Homer, the *Illiad* and the *Odyssey*.

This poem, which is a description of all of the signs
of the heavens (of the zodiac) is quoted in the New
Testament in Acts 17:28, where Paul says: **"For in him
we live, and move, and have our being; as certain also
of your own poets have said, For we are also his
offspring."** That is a quote from *Diosemeia*. Just a few
lines later, Aratus says in that same poem (and he is
attributing all of this to Zeus, who was the head of the
Greek pantheon of gods): "Since he himself hath fixed
in heaven these signs . . ."

A chart of the zodiac shows twelve major signs around
the ecliptic which was the apparent path that the sun
traveled through the heavens. Of course, the sun doesn't
travel in that circular path, but as the earth goes around
the sun, it projects the sun across the heavens and makes
it appear to do that.

To make it easier to understand, if you painted a picture of the whole sky on the ceiling, you would have a 360 degree circle. This is called the ecliptic. The ecliptic is divided into 12 houses, or mansions, or tabernacles for the sun. The sun travels around this ecliptic. Think of it as a great pie divided into 12 slices, each slice being 30 degrees of the 360 degrees. On the ecliptic there are 12 major constellations known as the constellations of the zodiac, or the signs of the zodiac.

In addition to the twelve major signs, there are also 36 decans. The word *decan* comes from the ancient root "deck," which means "a piece" or "to break in pieces." Thus there are the twelve major signs and 36 decans, or minor signs, that are connected with each of the twelve houses or mansions of the zodiac.

In each of these houses (or slices of the pie) there are not only major constellations on the ecliptic, but there are also three minor constellations which further explain the meaning of the symbols. So what we actually have is 12 major theses, each of which has three minor points under it.

As there were twelve apostles and twelve tribes of Israel, so there are these twelve chapters in the heavenly story. These twelve chapters are divided into three great books of four chapters each. These three books deal generally with that which has been accomplished in the past by Christ. The first two books deal with that which is taking place presently; the last book tells the story of the future consummation and judgment of the world. We are going to look at each of the twelve chapters individually as they relate to Christianity.

Prayer: How great thou art, Oh God, who hath painted the starry skies with a message of redemption and hath revealed unto men everywhere the story of the coming, the suffering, the death and resurrection of Thy Son. We thank Thee that we have it in all of its fullness in Thy Word today and pray that we, having the full revelation, may join with Thee in making a world that is blind and deaf, see and hear the wonders of Your grace. We ask it in Christ's name. Amen.

NOTE TO READERS: For your convenience, there is a foldout
chart of the Planisphere of the Heavens in the back of the book.

I. VIRGO

The Virgin

**For the invisible things of him from the creation
of the world are clearly seen, being understood by
the things that are made, even his eternal power
and Godhead; so that they are without excuse.**
                                        — Romans 1:20

Where do we begin to interpret this picture of the
zodiac, since a circle has neither beginning nor
ending? Modern astrology begins with *Aries,
The Lamb* (or the ram). But how do we know that is the
place to begin? Since everything else about it has been
corrupted, perhaps that is corrupted also. The fact is, it
has!

We may find the key to that riddle in the sphinx. I know
it will surprise you, but the sphinx actually unlocks the
mystery of the zodiac. It is fascinating to note that in
the Temple of Esneh in Egypt, there is a great sky-
painting in the portico on the ceiling which shows the
whole picture of the zodiac with all of its constellations.
Between the figures of *Virgo, The Virgin,* and *Leo, The
Lion,* there is carved the figure of the sphinx with the
head of a woman and the body of a lion. The woman's
face is looking at the virgin and the lion's tail is pointing
at Leo, telling us that we begin with the virgin and end
with Leo.

That same sphinx is found in the same place in a number
of other great paintings of the Mazzaroth (or the
constellations of the zodiac), in other parts of the Near
East, going back as much as 4,000 years, telling us the
original place of beginning.

So we will begin our study with the first house whose major sign is *Virgo*, and is depicted as a woman. You can look at the stars in *Virgo* until you are green in the face and they would never look like a woman! But the picture which has gone with them down through the ages, in every nation in the world, is a picture of a woman, and she is clearly identified as a virgin.

She is called Bethulah (Hebrew), which means "virgin." *Virgo* also means "virgin" in Latin, Greek and Arabic. Aratus, in 270 B.C., in one of the lines of his poem says, "Beneath Bootes' feet the virgin seek." (On the zodiac she is found beneath the feet of the constellation *Bootes*.) Everywhere in every language it is very clear that this is not merely a woman, but this is a virgin.

We are again reminded of the *protoevangelium*, that **"the seed of the woman would destroy the seed of the serpent,"** and of the great text in Isaiah 7:14: **"Behold! A virgin shall conceive, and bear a son."** That is, of course, a picture of Mary, the virgin mother of Christ.

Therefore, the second thing we note about the sign of *Virgo* is the emphasis upon her fertility (her motherhood), because she holds in her right hand a branch and in her left hand some sheaves of corn, or seeds of wheat. There are various interpretations given concerning that. As Christians we can easily see here a reference to the seed of the woman (that is, the virgin) who will conceive and bring forth a child (Isaiah 7:14).

A number of times the Scripture refers to Jesus as "The Branch." **"Behold the man whose name is The BRANCH" (Zechariah 6:12).** That is one of the names in the Old Testament for the coming of the Messiah. Also, concerning the Branch, we read in Zechariah 3:8, **"For, behold, I will bring forth my servant the BRANCH."** Also

"In that day shall the branch of the LORD be beautiful and glorious" (Isaiah 4:2a). He is the servant, He is a man, He is God; He is the God-man servant, Jesus, who has come.

In the other hand of the *Virgo, The Virgin* there are sheaves of corn, reminding us of the fact that it is the seed of the woman. Jesus used the figure "the seed of corn," which unless it falls into the ground and dies, abideth alone.

So we have a twofold testimony: the Virgin is going to bring forth the Branch which will be the Seed of the woman. A confirmatory of this is that the brightest star in *Virgo* is called *Spica*, which has the ancient meaning of "The Branch"—a picture of the coming of Christ. If that is not conclusive enough, a study of all the major and minor constellations would make the meaning absolutely clear.

Coma, The Desired

Let us now look at the three decans or other pieces of *Virgo's* house. The first one is called *Coma*. It depicts a woman sitting in a chair holding a child in her arms. This *Coma* means the "Desired One," or "Longed for One." It talks about the **"desire of all nations"** who should come: Jesus Christ.

We are told in ancient tradition that the star of Bethlehem was in the constellation *Coma*. Tradition also tells us that Zoroaster, the Persian religious leader, was a student of Daniel when he was in Babylon. He learned from Daniel that a star would appear in the constellation *Coma* when that One whom it foretold was to be born. That may or may not be the case, but we do know very conclusively that it is indicating a virgin woman with a son. In fact, the name for the sign *Coma* in the Egyptian language is *Shes-nu*, which means "The Desired Son."

Here we have an interesting example of how these signs have been corrupted in a few cases down through the centuries, for if you look at modern star maps of this, you will not find a woman with a child, but a woman's wig. How did that happen? To find out we have to go all the way back to a certain queen by the name of Berenice, who was the wife of Ptolemy III, King of Egypt in the 3rd century B.C. Her brother went out on a dangerous expedition and she made a vow to Venus that if he returned alive and in good health, she would devote or give her magnificent head of hair to Venus.

He did return and she did have her locks clipped and hung up in the temple of Venus where her wig subsequently was stolen. However a certain famous Egyptian astronomer by the name of Conon, who lived from 283 to 222 B.C. in Alexandria, Egypt, reported that Jupiter himself had taken this wig and had made it into a constellation, now called *Coma Berenice*. (The Greeks did not know how to translate it and substituted their own word for hair, *Co-me*, and called it *Berenice's Hair*.)

However, if you go back to any of the ancient zodiacs prior to the 3rd century B.C., you will find nothing about a wig, but rather, you will find a woman seated on a chair holding a child in her arms. Interestingly, Shakespeare even knew the real meaning of *Coma* for he speaks of the shooting of an arrow up "to the good boy in *Virgo's* lap."

An Arabian astronomer, Albumazar, one of the great gatherers of all the ancient knowledge about astronomy that has come down to us today, said, "There arises in the first decan, as the two Hermes and Aescalius teach, a young woman, whose Persian name translated into Arabic is *Adrenedefa*, a pure and immaculate virgin, holding in the hand two ears of corn, sitting on a throne, nourishing an infant, in the act of feeding him, who has a Hebrew name (the boy, I say) by some nations called Ihesu . . . which we in Greek call Christ"!!!!

That was a statement made by a non-Christian Arabian astronomer of the 8th century named Albumazar!

So in this first constellation, *Coma*, we have a picture of a woman who is a virgin, who is going to bring forth a Seed, who is to be called a Branch, and He is the **"desire of all nations" (Haggai 2:7a)**, the desired Son of God who was to come. Here we have the *protoevangelium*, the first promised Gospel.

Centaurus, The Centaur

The second decan is *Centaurus, The Centaur*—part horse and part man. We are reminded here that this One who was to come (who was first prophesied as the Seed) has come, and is seen as the infant boy being nourished in the lap of the virgin, but is now a man. However he is a very unusual man. He is a man having two natures: part man and part horse. The Hebrew name for this is *Bezeh*, which means "the despised one." Isaiah 53 uses this term twice: **"He is despised and rejected of men . . . he was despised, and we esteemed him not" (Isaiah 53:3).**

Although the original meaning of this sign became corrupted, as it went out and combined itself with the ignorance and the mythology and the paganism of the various people, the original meaning still shines through.

For example, in Greek mythology centaurs were heaven-begotten. They were born of the clouds; they were sons of the gods. But they were hated and abhorred by both gods and men. They were combatted, driven to the mountains, and finally exterminated.

The most famous centaur, and the head of all of the centaurs in Greek mythology, was called Cheiron, who was renowned for his hunting, for medicine, for music, for teaching and for prophecy. He was thought to be immortal. But, he voluntarily agreed to die and transferred his immortality to Prometheus. Here we see a picture of the Christ who was to come: the great Teacher, the great Healer, the great Prophesier, who, though immortal, gave up His life and transferred His immortality to others.

In the decan *Centaurus*, he is pictured going forth as a hunter with a spear and is slaying a beast called the *Victim*. We find Christ slaying Himself, as a victim, on a cross. Is that not what we have in the Scripture? **"No man taketh it [my life] from me, but I lay it down of myself. I have power to lay it down, and I have power to take it again" (John 10:18).** Did not Jesus Christ as the great High Priest offer Himself as the Final Evening Sacrifice? Here is incredible confirmation of all of this; the two natures of Christ are seen in the slaying of the victim, the sacrifice for the sins of man.

Bootes, The Coming One

The final decan in this house is *Bootes*, which is right next to *Coma*. It is a picture of a man moving forward. From the way his legs are placed, you can see that he is coming forward rapidly. In one hand he holds a spear; in the other hand, over his head, he holds a sickle.

The Egyptians called him *Smat*, which means "One Who Rules, Subdues, and Governs." The name Bootes comes from the Hebrew root word *Bo* which means "To Come." He is "The Coming One." Another name for this constellation is Arcturus which means "He Cometh."

So we see that this Savior comes now to rule, to subdue and to govern. He comes as a great Conqueror. In his head is a star. The astronomers call it *Beta* but the name of it is *Nekkar*, which means "The Pierced." We see also that the Pierced One is coming to be the judge and the conqueror and harvester of the earth. In Revelation 14:15 we have a picture of Christ coming to judge the world. In his right hand he has a sharp-edged sickle with which He is going to harvest the earth and bring forth men and women unto the Final Judgment.

In Summary. . .

In this first of the twelve books of the zodiac, you will notice that what we have is a great celestial preaching of the Gospel. We have, first of all, the woman promised in the *protoevangelium*: the Seed of the woman who is going to destroy the seed of the serpent. We have *Virgo*, the virgin woman, holding the branch and seeds in her hand. We find next to her, *Coma*, "The Desired One" (the Desire of all nations, who shall come), who is now an infant being nourished in her lap. Thirdly, we see him grown to manhood (*Centaurus*), a very unusual man: one with two natures; one who is the great hunter, teacher, physician; one who gives his life voluntarily and conveys his immortality to others; one who is the great High Priest, slaying the victim over the Southern Cross.

Finally, we see him full grown, coming mightily in power, as *Bootes*—"The Coming One," "The Ruler," "the

Governor," "the Harvester of the Earth" with a sickle in his hand, in judgment, to harvest the world.

Even as in Genesis we have an overview of the whole message of salvation, so, also, we have in this first book of the heavenly proclamation of the Gospel, a picture of Christ in His prophesied coming as the Seed of the virgin, in His birth and nativity, in His suffering and priesthood, and finally, in His coming in glory and judgment as the harvester of the earth. It is the glorious proclamation of the birth, sufferings, and future glory of Jesus Christ our Lord.

I hope that as you go out and look at the starry skies above you will be impressed anew and afresh. As we proceed with the signs, you will become amazed at the God who has written on high these things for all the world to see. For surely His voice has gone unto the ends of the earth, and the invisible things of Him from the creation of the world are plainly seen, as God has placed these constellations which He brings forth with His own hand in its season—pictures of the great salvation which He has wrought in Jesus Christ.

Prayer: Our Father, we thank Thee that Thou hath left no one in ignorance. We thank Thee that Thou hath given us Thy Word to make clear again the teaching of Thy Gospel. But we praise Thee that during those many centuries, when there was no written Gospel, that Thou hath not left Thyself without witness but hath proclaimed Thy glory and Thy salvation in the starry skies above. We rejoice that Thou art the Sovereign Lord who telleth all of the stars, who numbereth them and calleth them by name, and bringeth them forth in their order, and hath used them to declare Thy glory unto mankind; even the glory of Thy gracious salvation through the Seed of the woman, our great Savior, Deliverer and Judge, even Jesus Christ the Lord. Amen.

II. LIBRA

The Scales

Let this mind be in you, which was also in Christ Jesus: Who, being in the form of God, thought it not robbery to be equal with God: But made himself of no reputation, and took upon him the form of a servant, and was made in the likeness of men: And being found in fashion as a man, he humbled himself, and became obedient unto death, even the death of the cross. Wherefore God also hath highly exalted him, and given him a name which is above every name: That at the name of Jesus every knee should bow, of things in heaven, and things in earth, and things under the earth; And that every tongue should confess that Jesus Christ is Lord, to the glory of God the Father.

— Philippians 2:5-11

Having previously dealt with *Virgo, The Virgin,* we now come in our series to the second house or mansion in the zodiac: *Libra, The Scales.*

We will begin with the major sign in the second house. In Latin *Libra* means "The Scales"; in Hebrew it is *Mozanaim,* "The Scales Weighing." We are reminded of the verse in Scripture: **"Thou art weighed in the balances [scales], and art found wanting"** (Daniel 5:27). In *Libra* we see two scales, one higher and one lower. These scales represent the whole theme of redemption, or purchase, and describe a commercial transaction. Many people might ask what commercial transaction has to do with Christianity. My friends, it is at the very *heart* of Christianity.

We come to celebrate the redemption of Jesus Christ. But what does redemption mean? It comes from the Latin *emptio* which means "To Buy" or "To Purchase" and the prefix "re." In the word *redemtio* the "d" is put in merely for euphony so that there are not two "e's" in a row. *Redemtio* or redemption means "To Purchase Back." Christ has bought back those who come under the debt of sin. **"He . . . redeemed them from the hand of the enemy" (Psalms 106:10).** It means to pay the price, to ransom, to purchase back that which was lost. Christ is the great Redeemer. In Libra, as peculiarly set before us, is the whole theme of redemption.

There are three bright stars in this constellation which tell, I believe, the whole story. For example, the brightest star in the lower scale is entitled *Zuben al Genubi* which means "The Price Deficient." It is a picture of a man weighed in the scales and found wanting; man, ruined and condemned; man, with his life added up and found wholly in vanity and wholly wanting and insufficient to meet the requirements of God.

In the upper scale there is another bright star which is called *Zuben al Chemali* which means "The Price Which Covers." Jesus Christ is the price which covers. When Christ is placed in the scales, then we have that weight which indeed causes us to be acceptable in the sight of God.

In Revelation 5 we read: **"And they sung a new song, saying, Thou art worthy . . . for thou wast slain, and hast redeemed us to God by thy blood."** Christ is the glorious Redeemer who has purchased us with His own blood on the cross.

Another interesting star located just outside the bottom of the lower scale is called *Zuben Akrabi*, which means

"The Price of the Conflict," and refers to the cost of the "Price Which Covers." It signifies how much it cost Christ the Redeemer to purchase that covering for us. We see that this commercial transaction is at the very heart of the Gospel of Jesus Christ who purchased us back by His own blood from the realm of death and sin and Satan.

In some of the ancient pictures of the zodiac it is interesting that the lower scale is held in the claw of the Scorpion, the Scorpion being one of several pictures of Satan. This is a picture of mankind held in the grip of Satan.

Let us consider the three decans of this particular house of *Libra*. Keep in mind that what we are seeing here is the preaching of the Gospel as it was written by the hands of God in the heavens above; that the book of nature and the book of Scripture were written by the same divine hand. Therefore, it would come as no great surprise to discover that they are both telling the same divine story about the same Divine Redeemer. I trust that as this unfolds and develops before your eyes, you might see the glory of the Gospel in a new and more lustrous light and see, indeed, that the Bible obviously is here proclaimed again to be the Word of God as it is found in conformity to the everlasting stars in the heavens above.

Crux, The Southern Cross

The first of the decans in the house of *Libra* is *The Cross (Crux)*, "The Southern Cross." It is situated beneath the feet of the Centaur. This is one of the most beautiful of signs in the heavens and one where the stars, indeed, look like the picture which they portray: a cross. It is found in the very lowest part of the sphere and in the darkest part of the heavens. It may be seen by those dwelling near or south of the equator. Due to the precession of the equinoxes, the Southern Cross is sometimes visible and sometimes not, at different times and centuries.

In Hebrew this decan is called *Adom*, which means "The Cutting Off." In Daniel 9:26 we read: **"After threescore and two weeks shall Messiah be cut off."** Here we have the connection of the Messiah with the crux or the cross; the "cutting off" of the Messiah.

It is interesting that this constellation, though it is now far to the south from the latitude of Jerusalem, had been seen there for many centuries, but disappeared from view at almost exactly the time that Christ, the real Sacrifice, died on the cross. It has not been seen there since! In fact, it was not until the 16th century, when men sailed into the South Seas and around the Cape of Africa, that reports again came back of having seen this glorious constellation. From ancient records, Dante had spoken and written about the glorious Cross which had never been seen except by the eyes of the early race of men. So in the 16th century men were greatly moved when they saw this constellation they had heard and read of, but which had not been seen in well over a thousand years.

Victima, The Victim

The second decan in this particular house of *Libra* is called *Victima, The Victim*. It is located right below the scales. It is a picture of an animal, sometimes called today in Latin, *Lupus, The Wolf*. The ancient Greeks called it merely *Thera*, which meant simply a beast of some sort, not necessarily a wolf. The earliest Arabian figures show the victim as *Sura, The Lamb*. At the famous Dendereh zodiac it is portrayed as a child. We know that Scripture calls Christ ". . . **the Lamb slain from the foundation of the world" (Revelation 13:8).**

Whatever we call *The Victim*, it is an animal, a beast, seen in the act of falling over dead with the spear of the two-natured One. We have already seen this as Christ piercing its heart. The ancient Hebrew name *Asedah*, as well as the Arabic *Asedaton*, both mean *To Be Slain*.

Not only was Christ crucified, He was crucified, dead, and buried. Beyond the cross there is the slain and dead body of the Victim. Again, let me point out that I think it is fascinating that both the Victim *(Sura)* the lamb, the animal, the sacrifice, is *Christ*, and the one who is putting Him to death is Christ. We should remember the words of Christ Himself: **"I lay down my life for the sheep . . . No man taketh it [my life] from me . . . I have power to lay it down, and I have power to take it again" (John 10:15,18).**

The Scripture says that He has put away sin by the sacrifice of Himself. The Old Testament Jews knew that Christ was going to be a great high Priest who would offer a sacrifice for sin, but they never dreamed that the sacrifice He would offer was the High Priest Himself. And yet, that picture has been there in the sky for many centuries—if they had only seen and truly understood.

The names of the constellations came to be distorted by pagan religions. The Egyptians, for example, called the *Victim, Horus*, "The Coming One," who was portrayed not as an animal but as a youth, the son of Osiris and the Virgin. He had his finger over his mouth as if signaling silence. The Greeks and Romans called him *Harpocrates*, meaning "Justice" or, the "Victim of Justice," or the "Vindication of Majestic Law." Among the Romans, *Harpocrates* was known as the god of silence or quiet submission.

We are reminded that the Scripture tells us "... **as a sheep before her shearers is dumb, so he [Christ] openeth not his mouth" (Isaiah 53:7b).** He came quietly and submissively to offer Himself, which is symbolized by the finger over His lips. All of this simply fills out the picture we have of Christ as the silent, submissive Sufferer; the Lamb of God who gave Himself up to death, to suffer for the sins of the people.

Corona, The Crown

The third decan of this particular house of *Libra* is known as *Corona* or *Cornone Borealis, The Crown* or *The Northern Crown*.

Our text states: **"Who [Christ], being in the form of God, thought it not robbery to be equal with God: But made himself of no reputation ... And being found in fashion as a man, he humbled himself, and became obedient unto death, even the death of the cross. Wherefore God also hath highly exalted him, and given him a name which is above every name" Philippians 2:6-9).** Christ is the crowned Victor, the one who has triumphed over death and Satan and the grave. He is the one who has crushed the serpent beneath His feet; the one who now is the great ruling Redeemer of the world.

It is interesting that each chapter (each sign, each mansion, each house in the zodiac) ends its final decan in one of glory; one of victory; one of triumph, either for Christ or for his followers! In the same way, we see that the Bible, with the book of Revelation, ends with the great triumph and victory of Jesus Christ.

For example, in the first house of *Virgo*, the final decan *Bootes* represents "The Coming One," "The Conqueror," "The Harvester," coming to harvest the world in judgment. For unbelievers, that means death and terror and condemnation and wrath. But for believers it means to be received into the presence of God, to receive our rewards, and to enter into paradise forever.

We see here the final decan of *Libra* is *The Crown* which Jesus Christ won by His death, as He has been highly exalted by God. The Scripture says, **"But we see Jesus ... for the suffering of death, crowned with glory and honour" (Hebrews 2:9).** And so we rise from the cross and from the slain *Victim* to that One whom God has raised from the dead, taken up into heaven, and caused to sit at His right hand, crowned with honor and glory.

In Arabic this constellation is known as *Al Iclil*, which means "An Ornament" or "Jewel." We talk about the stars which make up the crown of Jesus Christ and how we are part of the stars in His crown. The brightest star in that particular constellation of *Corona, The Crown*, is called *Al Phecca* which means "The Shining." So we end up with a picture of a crown of jewels shining brightly in the northern sky. Christ has risen from the depths of the *Southern Cross*, all the way up to the heights of the *Northern Crown* and is now crowned in glory and honor.

We are also reminded here of the fact that there is a crown which is offered unto us. Jesus Christ says in the book of Revelation: **"be thou faithful unto death, and I will give thee a crown of life" (Revelation 2:10).** Without a cross there is not a crown. We are called to take up our cross and to follow Him—to be faithful followers of Christ.

Look up into the night sky and see the Northern Crown, the *Corona Borealis* (which, by the way, shines at midnight every night over the city of Jerusalem) and be reminded that there is a crown for those who are faithful to Jesus Christ. Those who follow Him daily in their lives will be brought to sit upon the throne and will be highly exalted with Him.

And, as you look up into the sky at night and see the heavens sparkling with stars, I hope that a new sense of wonder and a new element of faith will be added as you realize that the hand that inscribed those stars in the sky is the same hand that has drawn in the Scripture the plan of salvation. It is the same Savior who was born at Bethlehem and died on a cross and now reigns in glory above—the One who one day we shall see face to face.

Prayer: Father, we pray that Thy Holy Spirit will continue to strengthen our faith in the glory and wonder of Thy great redemption which is writ in Scripture and writ above in the starry skies for all to see. Cause our hearts to swell with joy and our souls to rejoice at Thy goodness in the wondrous revelation which Thou has given to all of the world and for the redemption accomplished by Jesus Christ upon the cross. We make this prayer in His most holy name. Amen.

III. SCORPIO

The Scorpion

And the great dragon was cast out, that old serpent,
called the Devil, and Satan, which deceiveth the
whole world: he was cast out into the earth, and
his angels were cast out with him.

—Revelation 12:9

In this third chapter of the Gospel gallery in the
heavens entitled *Scorpio, The Scorpion*, we move to
the very heart of the Gospel, to the very heart of the
protoevangelium: the battle between Christ and the
serpent.

A scorpion is a most malignant insect. It is indeed a
noisome, dangerous pest and one that is very frightening.
Although the bite is not always fatal, it can be, and it
is always extraordinarily painful.

The picture attached to this constellation is that of a
giant scorpion which is larger than a man. If a little insect
puts fear in the heart of a large man, how much more
so would a scorpion, who is eight, ten, or twelve feet long.
That would put the fear of God into anyone!

But here we have a giant scorpion, *Scorpio*, as he is
called from the Latin, and *Scorpious* from the Greek. In
Arabic and Syriac, this constellation is known as *Al
Akrab* which means "Scorpion," but it also means "The
Conflict," or "War." Here we go to the very heart of the
whole message of the Bible. And what is that message?
Essentially, it is about a great warfare. And though that
warfare is often portrayed as the battle between the forces
of righteousness and the forces of evil in this world—
between faith and unbelief; between the followers of Christ
and the followers of anti-Christ—ultimately, it is a battle

between Christ and Satan. It all began in that battle in heaven.

The first half of the book of Revelation describes this battle in light of the various followers of Christ and Satan. But beginning with the 12th chapter the principal antagonist and protagonist are brought to light, and we see the woman bringing forth the man-child who is to rule the nations: that child is Christ. We also see there the revelation of that old serpent, the dragon, which is Satan. We read in the Scripture: **"And the great dragon was cast out, that old serpent, called the Devil, and Satan, which deceiveth the whole world: he was cast out into the earth" (Revelation 12:9).** This dragon (or serpent) is described in many ways in the Bible. For example, in Revelation 9:10,11, he is described this way: **"And they had tails like unto scorpions, and there were stings in their tails: and their power was to hurt men five months. And they had a king over them, which is the angel of the bottomless pit, whose name in the Hebrew tongue is Abaddon, but in the Greek tongue hath his name Apollyon."** And so we see that the king of these scorpions, that scorpion himself whose sting is in his tail, is Apollyon—another name for Satan.

In the Coptic language this constellation is called *Isidis*, meaning "Attack of the Enemy." The names of the stars themselves, which come from Babylonian, Persian, and Coptic antiquity (though principally from the Arabic), also add meaning to the constellations.

The principal star in this constellation of *Scorpio* is its brightest and most well known star, *Antares*, which is right at the heart of *Scorpio*. This ancient Arabic name is thought by some to mean "The Wounding" (cutting or tearing), which is precisely what the scorpion is designed to do. He comes to wound and kill, as Jesus said.

There is another bright star in the tail of *Scorpio* known by the name of *Lesath*, (Hebrew), and means "The Perverse." It signifies Satan's perverse nature and how he would rebel against God, who had made him the brightest of all of his angels. Satan perversely determined to destroy God's kingdom, His followers, and His power.

So here we have a picture of this great *Scorpion* and a blueprint of his battle with Christ. The serpent (or scorpion, or Satan), throughout all Scripture, has been the enemy that was attacking Christ. For example, Pharaoh tried to destroy all of the "Children" of the Hebrews in order that the line leading to the Messiah might be cut off. Athaliah destroyed all the royal seed of Israel, but the king's son was rescued. In the book of Esther, Haman tried to destroy all of the Jews, and yet he was put to rout by Esther and they were saved. Again, at Bethlehem, Herod killed all of the babies under two years of age in an attempt to destroy the Christ child. In Revelation chapter 12, we read that when the woman brought forth her son, the devil (the dragon, that old serpent) was there waiting to try to destroy Christ.

So here is *Scorpio, The Scorpion.* Jesus had His struggles with him—struggles which climaxed in Gethsemane, the "hour of the powers of darkness," said Christ. There he felt something more of the sting, but principally, there upon the cross of Calvary, the scorpion plunged his stinger deep into Jesus Christ and brought Him down into the grave. But, as we know, Christ rose again from the grave and conquered the scorpion. All of the parts of this mansion, or house in the zodiac, deal with this central struggle of the Scripture.

Orphiuchus, The Serpent-Holder

We come now to the first of the three decans of this particular chapter. The Greek name by which this figure is commonly known is *Orphiuchus* which simply means "The Serpent- Holder." It portrays a great man struggling with a giant serpent who is trying to keep him from accomplishing what he is attempting to do. The serpent is reaching up to grasp the crown, even as Satan in the Old Testament sought to lift himself to be equal with and take the place of God.

In fact, out of jealousy against God, this has always been Satan's intent, and this is what he tries to get his followers to do. He said, **"Ye shall be as gods" (Genesis 3:5)**. Even today, in humanism, man attempts to take the place of God so that he will have dominion. But we see that *Orphiuchus, The Serpent-Holder*, is restraining the serpent, preventing him from achieving that triumph. Here is the strong man who is overcoming the evil one.

Coming out of the Arabic into the Greek, the name of *Orphiuchus* is Aesculapius. Aesculapius was one of the favorite of the Greek gods, a son of Apollo. Homer describes Aesculapius with all of the attributes of a man. He was a god-man. If you read of the death of Socrates as described by Plato, you will notice the last request Socrates makes is to ask Crito, his friend, to repay a cock he owes to Aesculapius. Here was a god who was much on the mind of the great Socrates, even at the moment of his death.

According to Greek mythology, he was the healer: he cured the sick. He was also reported to bring the dead back to life by means of blood taken from the side of the goddess of justice. He is called the "Physician," "The Desired One," "The Health-Giver," the "Universal

Remedy." Finally, he suffered death from the lightnings of heaven, but was raised from death to glory through the influence of his father, Apollo.

Now we can see how this original revelation began to be corrupted as the pagan nations lost sight of the original revelation that God has given, and began to destroy and change and twist these things. But it does not take a great deal of wisdom or imagination to see the light of the original glory through the distortion coming from paganism.

Christ, the coming Savior of the world, is revealed. He is the Great Physician who cures various diseases, who heals the minds and bodies and souls of those who appeal unto Him, who brings life out of death by blood taken from the side of the goddess of justice. Jesus took upon Himself the sins of mankind, suffered in our stead the penalty that we deserve and justice demands, and through the shedding of blood which came from His side, He is able to raise the dead.

Finally Aesculapius dies as the lightning bolts of heaven descend upon him. This is a picture of the fact that Christ, having had imputed upon Him the sins of the world, now also suffers the Father's wrath. The very lightning bolts of heaven descend upon Him and are discharged into His body, and Christ endures in His own body and soul the infinite penalty and wrath of God the Father, who could say, **"This is my beloved Son, in whom I am well pleased" (Matthew 3:17)**. Yet, because of His love for us, God gave Him up to that great disaster upon Calvary. But He was not left in the tomb; He was raised to glory. Indeed He shall heal the nations for He has defrauded the tomb with His victory.

Serpens, The Serpent

The second decan in *Scorpio* is *Serpens, The Serpent*, which Aesculapius (or Orphiuchus) is holding. Again we see this serpent theme repeated over and over in the zodiac. In fact, a great astronomer who did not understand this, said: "Why, the whole heavens are scribbled over with serpents and snakes," echoing most astronomers' disdain for astrology. The devil is portrayed as the great antagonist in this battle. He is portrayed as a serpent; as a dragon; as a scorpion; as Cetus, the water-snake; and as Hydra, the many-headed monstrous snake. He is presented in many guises, but always as a malignant, venomous and hostile creature.

Here we see the Serpent attempting to gain the crown. But we see that he is held and restrained by Christ. In Revelation chapter 20, we see that Christ takes that serpent and binds him, casts him down, and locks him up. Christ is the One who is able to restrain the power of the serpent.

It is interesting that in the Gospel According to St. Luke, we read that Christ gives to us the power which He gained at Calvary. The great victories He has accomplished He now gives over to those who would be His followers. Later, in Luke 10:19, Christ says, **"Behold, I give unto you power to tread on serpents and scorpions, and over all the power of the enemy: and nothing shall by any means hurt you."** Imagine: power to tread upon serpents and scorpions! In this house of the zodiac, both of these are clearly depicted. Furthermore, the victory which Christ won over Satan is ours, even as the passage in Revelation goes on to say that we **"conquer by His blood and by our testimony of our faith in Him."**

Hercules, The Mighty One

The third decan in this particular house is *Hercules*. It describes more fully the working out of the Gospel. Because the pagan nations had lost sight of this original revelation, they began to assign different people to the various figures and the men portrayed in these constellations. What they really depict, in fact, is Christ in His various offices and His various functions, accomplishing some of the many-sided tasks He came into this world to accomplish.

Hercules is seen upside down, immediately over *Orphiuchus*, on a planisphere. *Scorpio* was getting ready to sting *Orphiuchus* on his left heel, but with his right foot, *Orphiuchus* is ready to crush *Scorpio*. As the *protoevangelium* said, the serpent would wound his heel, but he would wound its head and give him the mortal wound from which he would never recover.

We see this more fully described for us in the case of *Hercules*. In Hebrew, the constellation *Hercules* is called *Gibbor*, which means "Mighty." Thus, *Hercules* means "The Mighty One." In Isaiah 9:6, we read: **"For unto us a child is born, unto us a son is given . . . and his name shall be called Wonderful, Counsellor, The mighty God . . ."** In Hebrew, the mighty God is *El Gibbor*. Here again is another picture of Christ, not as the healer *Aesculapius*, who indeed restrains the venomous destructive and sickening power of the serpent; but as the hero-God—*El-Gibbor* who destroys the power of the enemy.

Hercules is shown down on one knee with a mighty club raised over his head. One of the stars in this figure means "The Head of Him Who Bruises"—the one who comes to bruise. *Hercules* has in his hand *Cerberus*, the three-headed monster that guarded the gates into hell— another picture of Satan. Christ is the One who descended into hell. Even as Samson ripped off the gates and took them to the top of the hill and cast them away, so Christ is the One who has gone down into hell, has destroyed the power of Satan, has led captivity captive, has taken the Old Testament saints out of Sheol and led them up into the very presence of God (where Christ is the great Hero, the *Gibbor*, who is about to destroy the three-headed monster). It is another picture of Satan as the one who holds the people in the dark pit of hell and has come to bruise that "One."

By the way, though this goes outside of this particular chapter or house, a planisphere shows the foot of Hercules on the top of the head of the dragon. That brings us back to the Scripture that describes Satan as "that old serpent," "the scorpion," "the dragon." All three of these are descriptive of the power of Satan. Over the scorpion, over the serpent and over the dragon, Christ, as both the healer of the nations and the destroyer of Satan, is the conqueror over all the works of Satan. Christ said that He came into the world to destroy the works of Satan.

The brightest star in this figure is located in the forehead of *Hercules* and is called *Ras-Al-Gethi*, "The Head of Him Who Bruises." Christ is the One who came to bruise the seed of the serpent.

The second brightest star in *Hercules* means "The Branch Kneeling." This takes us back to *Virgo*, who has a branch in one of her hands. We are reminded that the name of this One who is to come to redeem the world is the Branch, the One that would spring forth.

The Phoenicians worshipped Hercules as a savior who would come to deliver them. The Greeks called him *Herakles*, and they worshipped him as the greatest of their hero-gods, principally because of what are called the "Twelve Labors of Hercules." To them, he was a god-begotten man. Again, we see that there is something different. Hercules was not simply a god, he was not simply a man, rather he was a "God-begotten" man.

Throughout all of his life, this mythological character was engaged in the most difficult and wonderful of feats— "The Twelve Labors." Included among them are: vanquishing the many-headed Hydra and cleansing the Augean stables. I think that it is suggestive, indeed, that one of the great feats of Hercules was cleansing the Augean stables where thousands and thousands of animals were kept, but none of the stables had ever been cleaned! The filth and the stench must have been unbelievable, and yet, one of the tasks of Hercules was to clean the Augean stables!

There was, however, a greater stench. The Bible says we are a "stench in the nostrils of God" because of our sin; we have spiritual "B.O." and only Christ can take that away—only He can cleanse the stench of our Augean stable. Interestingly, Christ was born in a stable and came for the purpose of cleansing our stables.

As He was born in the stable of Bethlehem, so He is willing to be born in the stables of our heart. Hercules diverted a river to cleanse the Augean stables. Our "Greater-Than-Hercules" did not use water, but rather with His own precious blood He has cleansed the stable of innumerable millions of hearts of those who have trusted in Him.

Hercules also slew the three-headed snakelike monster, which is seen in his hands, and the dragon which guarded the golden apples of Hesperides. And so it was with Satan (the serpent), who, by his beguiling deceits tempted Adam and Eve to eat of the fruit from the tree of the knowledge of good and evil, that they might not have eternal life. And Christ, by destroying Satan, allows us not the golden apples of the Hesperides; rather, He allows us the very tree of life itself, the fruits of which bring life eternal to those who eat.

A Gallery of Truth

We see that beyond all the pagan distortions or confusions there is the clear revelation of the great central work of our God and Savior. It is a magnificent thing to see that in the unchanging stars of the heavens and the glorious signs placed there by God in the night sky, we have a gallery of evangelical truth, a picture of the great coming and conquering of Christ, our Savior and Lord.

We see that the hand that made those signs is divine. It is the same hand which has penned the revelation we have before us in our Scripture. It is the same story—ever old, ever new—of the Blessed Redeemer, the Seed of the Woman, the Son of the Virgin, the Savior of the world.

Prayer: Father, we thank Thee for the way in which Thou art able to bring forth in their seasons the Mazzaroth, the signs of the zodiac, the glorious portraits in the heavens which Thou, by thine own hand, hath painted. As Thou hath garnished the heavens with the glorious pictures of Thy triumph over Satan and the redemption of men, may we lift up our eyes and be amazed afresh at Thy grace and Thy glory. May we look down again into Thy Word, that we may see more fully the record of Thy love. We pray it in the name of Christ, our King. Amen.

IV. SAGITTARIUS

The Archer

Thine arrows are sharp in the heart of the king's enemies; whereby the people fall under thee. Thy throne, O God, is for ever and ever: the sceptre of thy kingdom is a right sceptre.

—Psalm 45:5,6

We come now in our study to the fourth chapter in this great heavenly epic: *Sagittarius*, the last chapter in the first book. He is a centaur: part man and part horse, and he is an archer. The word *Sagittarius* means "The Archer." In Akkadian, he is called *Nun-ki* which means "The Prince of the Earth." We see also that he has a dual nature.

This is the second centaur we have looked at in this study. The other one was in the first chapter of *Virgo.* He was also called a centaur and was in the process of giving himself up to die in the dual picture with *Lupus, The Victim.* (This depicts Christ, the despised one, slaying himself). But here in *Sagittarius* he is the victorious one—the risen and conquering king. He comes now as the *Archer*, not offering himself in sacrifice, but destroying Satan who made that sacrifice necessary.

The human portion of the *Centaur* is drawing a bow and aiming an arrow at *Atares*, the very heart of the *Scorpion.* An interesting statement that relates to this is found in Psalm 21:12, where we read, **"Therefore shalt thou make them turn their back, when thou shalt make ready thine arrows upon thy strings against the face of them."** The same thing is true in Psalm 45:5. **"Thine arrows are sharp in the heart of the king's enemies."** So here we see that Christ, the Conquering One, is the One whose arrow is aimed at the *Scorpion*.

Christ Coming in Glory

That this is a picture of Christ is made clear in Revelation 6:2 where we read of Christ coming forth in glory: **"And I saw, and behold a white horse: and he that sat on him had a bow; and a crown was given unto him: and he went forth conquering, and to conquer."** Here is that One who comes upon a white horse, who has a bow, and goes forth conquering and to conquer. The one who is conquered is, first of all, the leader of the host of all of the ungodly, namely—Satan, or the *Scorpion*. *Sagittarius* (Christ) is the conqueror of the *Scorpion*.

The Apostle Paul, in the Book of Acts, quotes from "Diosemeia" a great poem by Aratus, which sets the whole picture of the zodiac into verse. When Aratus comes to this section, he says **"Midst golden stars He stands refulgent now, and thrusts the Scorpion with his bended bow."** Here we find Christ in refulgent glory as the Conquering King coming forth upon a white horse with a bow.

The brightest star in *Sagittarius* is *Naim* which in Hebrew is "The Gracious (One)." This is exactly what we find in Psalm 45:2: **"Thou art fairer than the children of men: grace is poured into thy lips: therefore God hath blessed thee for ever."** So Christ, as we see here, is the Gracious One, as the star here named by God indicates that He is. Christ on the cross has conquered Satan and has crushed his head.

I think we ought to consider what that means for us. One of the questions thinking people have asked is: What kind of a world or what kind of a universe do we live in? Down through the centuries various answers have been given. For example, Zoroaster, one of the great ancient Persian prophets, thought that we lived in a universe where there was a god of good and a god of evil, and that they were perfectly balanced in the struggle that was going on. However, none knew what the outcome of that struggle would be.

On the other hand, there are the materialists today who believe that we live in a materialistic universe which ultimately will die. This heat-death of the second law of thermodynamics says:

- All collapses into entropy and the universe is totally indifferent to us.

- We have arisen by evolutionary chance and the universe could not care less.

- There is no power in this world but the power of natural forces, and they are totally indifferent to our welfare or to our hurt.

How different to realize that the universe we live in is a universe governed by a God who loves us, and that the evil power which exists in the world has been conquered by Christ. Of course there are some who believe in a universe where Satan reigns. Think how terrible it would be to live in a world where a malignant spirit truly reigns. How would you like to be a grasshopper in a bottle in the hands of a seven-year-old malicious boy? That is the kind of a universe some people think they live in!

But we have in *Sagittarius* a picture painted on the dome of heaven that tells us it is Christ, the One who loves us everlastingly, who has conquered Scorpio, and He is the One who rules over the world.

Lyra, The Harp

We now come to the three decans or minor points which exist in *Sagittarius*. The first one is *Lyra, The Harp*, or lyre, meaning "Praise for the Conqueror." *Lyra* is shown as a harp combined with an eagle or an eagle rising with a harp.

A very bright star in that particular constellation is *Vega*, a glittering gem in the night sky, and means "He Shall Be Exalted." Vega has been this star's name down through antiquity. It is the name which God Himself gave to it that He should be exalted—that Christ has come forth conquering and to conquer. What should be our response to that? Our response should be: *He shall be exalted!* It is interesting that this term is found in the song of Moses, after God overthrew the forces of Pharaoh in the Red Sea: **"I will sing unto the LORD, for he hath triumphed gloriously" (Exodus 15:1).**

The last verse of Psalm 21 talks about making ready for his arrows against the face of them and says, **"Be thou exalted, LORD, in thine own strength: so will we sing and praise thy power."** The very meaning of the star *Vega* is "He Shall Be Exalted." By His great power and might has He conquered; therefore, we are now to sing His praises.

The Bible tells us: **"And be not drunk with wine, wherein is excess; but be filled [constantly getting filled] with the Spirit . . . singing and making melody in your heart to the Lord" (Ephesians 5:18,19).** One of the ways you will know that a person is close to the Conquering Christ is that he is constantly singing and making melody in his heart; he is spending time with Christ, he has yielded himself to Christ, and has a song in his heart and joy in his soul.

The Scripture says, "... **at thy right hand there are pleasures [joy] for evermore" (Psalm 16:11b)**. I would ask you: What has been the testimony of your lips and of your heart? Are you singing and making melody to the Lord? Do you rejoice in Him? If by faith you claim His victory, then you are to sing His praises and the glory of His power.

Ara, The Altar

The second decan in this mansion of the zodiac is *Ara, The Altar*. It is illustrated as an altar. It is one of the southernmost constellations of the heavens and is turned downward. In fact, it is so far south that, though at one time in the past it could be seen from northern latitudes because of the precession of the equinoxes, it is no longer visible from this latitude. *Ara* means "Consuming Fire Prepared for His Enemies." It is seen as an altar or burning pyre, upside down pouring fire into the lower regions called *Tartarus*, or outer darkness.

This depicts that God, having conquered Satan, has prepared that place for Satan and his fallen angels—that place of consuming fire for him and all of those who follow him and have been deceived by him in this world. Again, in Psalm 21, this whole picture unfolds before us: **"Thine hand shall find out all thine enemies: thy right hand shall find out those that hate thee. Thou shalt make them as a fiery oven in the time of thine anger: the LORD shall swallow them up in his wrath, and the fire shall devour them" (Psalm 21: 8,9)**

We are told in II Thessalonians chapter 1, that Christ shall come with flaming fire, taking vengeance on those that believe not and obey not the Gospel of the Lord Jesus Christ. He shall come with His mighty angels to be glorified in all of those who do believe. It reminds us of the fact that we either take up the harp and the lyre and sing the praises of Christ, whom we have received as our Conquering King, or we become a part of the unbelievers, the unrepentant who have followed Satan (the Scorpion, that old dragon) and are cast into outer darkness and consumed with everlasting fire.

Think what it would mean to be cast out into that outer darkness, into those lower regions beyond the periphery of the heavens, beyond the horizon, beyond the equator, down into the lower depths, into darkness reserved for those who are impenitent forever.

The skeptics have liked to pretend that they have somehow evaporated hell. They think they have proven that it does not exist. My friends, nothing could be farther from the truth. There is not the slightest shred of evidence produced by them. They have mocked it; they have laughed at it; they have ridiculed it. But it still awaits them. Think what it would mean to wake up in outer darkness and to know that you would be there forever . . . forever . . . and forever! There is no thought more benumbing to the human mind than that.

But Jesus Christ, meek and mild, came to save us from our sin and from its consequences. He came that we may never know what lies beyond the horizon in the lower depths, in the outer darkness, in the *Tartarus* of God; in the burning altar and pyre of His consuming wrath. To do that, there on the cross He descended into the lower depths. He took all of our sin upon Himself. As horrible as it was, He endured its penalty for us.

Recently I spoke to a young lady on a plane. One of the first things she told me was that she didn't believe in hell. I said, "I do believe in hell. And the reason I believe in it is because Jesus Christ endured it for me on the cross. I know that it is real because I know that He suffered for me. I also can declare that it exists because I know that I'm not going there." She was struck by that statement and acknowledged that it was true . . . I'm happy to say that today she is no longer on her way over the horizon into the pit, but on her way to paradise.

Draco, The Dragon

The final decan in the final chapter in the first book of the zodiac ends with a picture of Satan being overwhelmed. In *Sagittarius*, this final decan is *Draco, The Dragon*. It is the dragon whose head is under the foot of Hercules.

As previously discussed, the last chapter in each of the three books of the zodiac ends with the victory of Christ and the destruction of Satan. The first book ends with *Draco, The Dragon*, being cast down; the second book ends with *Cetus, The Sea Monster*, Leviathan, being bound; the third one ends with *Hydra*, that old Serpent, being ultimately and finally destroyed.

It is interesting that many people say there is no devil. Someone has rightly said that if there is no devil, then someone is very busy going about doing his work for him! Certainly the work of Satan continues apace in our world today. If there is no Satan, how is it then that God has written so plainly across the sky the pictures of the serpent, the dragon, leviathan, and all of the other various pictures of Satan?

One astronomer said, "The heavens are scribbled over with serpents because Satan is very real." He is the great antagonist against whom Christ, the great protagonist, is set in mortal combat. Satan is the one that goes about deceiving mankind. His basic method of dealing with human beings is not the kind of things that we see portrayed in movies; it is simply through deceit that he works upon people. He is the father of lies, and is constantly trying to deceive people into thinking the wrong things. He tempts them by making them think "this will be better than that." He deludes humans into false religions by making them think they are true and deceives them into believing some pseudo-science, like evolution. But Christ is the great Victor over Satan and has finally destroyed him.

There is a beautiful picture of this in Revelation to which I would like to call your attention: **"And the great dragon was cast out, that old serpent, called the Devil, and Satan, which deceiveth the whole world: he was cast out into the earth, and his angels were cast out with him. And I heard a loud voice saying in heaven, Now is come salvation, and strength, and the kingdom of our God, and the power of his Christ: for the accuser of our brethren is cast down, which accused them before our God day and night. And they overcame him by the blood of the Lamb, and by the word of their testimony; and they loved not their lives unto the death" (Revelation 12:9-11).**

Draco, The Dragon is seen as a huge winding serpent, fierce, but firmly under the crushing foot of *Hercules*, who stands as a figure for the victorious Christ. In *Greek*, *Drakon* also means "Trodden Down." Here we see the *Dragon* as the one who is trodden on, which takes us back once again to the original *protoevangelium*, the first promise of Christ who would tread upon and bruise the head of the serpent.

The brightest star in this figure is called *Thuban* (Hebrew), and is located in the second coil from the tip of the serpent's tail. *Thuban* means "The Subtle." You will recall that in the Garden of Eden the serpent was more subtle than any of the beasts of the field. It is interesting to note that more than 4,700 years ago, shortly after the fall of man, *Thuban* was the pole star. But again, because of the precession of the equinoxes, that pole of the planet earth now points to Polaris and Satan has lost his preeminence because of the work of Christ.

In the serpent's head can be seen the bright star *Rastaban* (Hebrew), "The Head of the Subtle" or "The Head of the Serpent." The third brightest star bears the Hebrew name, *Ethanin*, "The Long Serpent" or "Dragon." Here the dragon is cast down, crushed, trodden on and overcome by the blood of the Lamb. Christ gains the victory!

Years ago my pastor said to me, "The devil is always trying to do one thing: he is trying to get rid of the blood of Christ. He is trying to get across some other kind of Gospel; trying to make Christianity out to be some sort of butcher shop religion." Satan always attacks the blood of Christ because it is His blood shed at Calvary which is the destruction of Satan, the remedy for sin, the secret of our regeneration and the hope of our eternal salvation. It is the blood of Christ claimed in the word of our testimony, which word must always be by the shed blood of Calvary.

I have been cleansed, I have been made anew: I have been redeemed. Once we understand what has been done for us at Calvary, and once that has become the testimony of our hearts and our lives, we will not love this life unto death. Satan tries to make people want to cling to this life above all and not see heaven in all of its glory and paradise in all of its wonderment. He does not want us to have the new body and the new life that God has prepared for us in His glorious city where the buildings and streets are made of transparent gold; where there is joy and peace and happiness; where there is no more pain, nor suffering, nor parting, nor sorrow, nor death.

Satan would like to make those things very vague and very faint and make this present life seem to us to be everything. But those who have truly come to know Christ and the power of His atoning death know that this life is but a faint shadow of the glory which is to come.

Prayer: Father, whether we look into Thy Word or lift our eye unto the glittering heavens, we see the same old, old story, but ever new, of the glory and grace of Jesus Christ, our Savior and Conquering King. Lord may our hearts yield themselves to Thee. If there be any who have never done so, may they say, "O Christ, thou Christ of the ages of Scripture, thou Christ of the night sky, come and be the Christ of my heart" In Thy name. Amen.

V. CAPRICORNUS

The Goat

And he shall take the two goats, and present them
before the LORD at the door of the tabernacle of
the congregation. And Aaron shall cast lots upon
the two goats; one lot for the LORD, and the other
lot for the scapegoat. And Aaron shall bring the
goat upon which the LORD'S lot fell, and offer him
for a sin offering. Then shall he kill the goat of
the sin offering, that is for the people, and bring
his blood within the veil, and do with that blood
as he did with the blood of the bullock, and sprinkle
it upon the mercy seat, and before the mercy seat:
And he shall make an atonement for the holy place
. . . because of their transgressions in all their sins:
and so shall he do for the tabernacle of the
congregation, that remaineth among them in the
midst of their uncleanness.

— Leviticus 16:7-9,15,16

We now come to the second of the three books.
Remember, we discussed the fact that the twelve
signs of the zodiac are divided into three books
with four signs in each book. The second book introduces
more fully the people of God and the work of Christ as
it relates to them.

The first sign of the second book is *Capricornus, The
Goat*. It is a picture of the Sea Goat. There is no prototype
of this strange creature, the front half of which is a goat
and the rear half a fish! But that is precisely what
Capricornus is.

What does it mean? The goat is in a fallen position
with one leg doubled under his body; the head is bent

forward and he is in a dying situation. On the other hand, the tail of the fish is vigorous and living. We have here a beautiful picture of what Christ accomplished by his death and that He brings forth out of His death the living body of His Church—referred to in Scripture as "fishes." In Hebrew the name of this constellation is *Gedi*, which means "A Kid; A Goat"; it also means "The Cut-Off"— again the picture and the meaning of atonement.

The picture and the meaning become even more clear as we consider some of the stars in this constellation. Some of the brightest stars are *Al Gedi*, which means "The Kid"; *Deneb Al Gedi*, "The Sacrifice Cometh"; *Ma'Asad*, "The Slaying." We see here a picture of the atoning sacrifice. The Scripture frequently has reference to goats as atoning sacrifices. In Leviticus 10:16,17 we read: **"And Moses diligently sought the goat of the sin offering . . . seeing it is most holy, and God hath given it you to bear the iniquity of the congregation, to make atonement for them before the LORD."**

Leviticus, Chapter 16, describes the great holy and high day of atonement. There we find not only the scapegoat that bears the sin of the people off into the wilderness, but the goat (the sin offering) which was taken by the high priest was slain, and its blood sprinkled upon the altar.

And so Christ is that great day of atonement. He is that great sin offering! He is the one who dies for us. Christ is both the Lamb of God and the Goat of God. We speak of the sheep and the goats. But the goat is usually spoken of in an adverse way. How is it then that Christ is referred to as a goat? This brings out the same great truth set forth in the Gospel of John: **"And as Moses lifted up the serpent in the wilderness, even so must the Son of man be lifted up"** (John 3:14). The goat is a picture of the sinful one. Jesus who is the spotless Lamb of God became sin for us. He was made a Goat for us, as the outcast one. There upon the cross, as the one cast out from God, He was bearing in Himself the iniquity of the world.

But out of His death proceeds light. From this dying goat, we also see a living fish. We see the thrashing tail of the fish as vigorous and alive. God's people in the Scripture are pictured as fishers of men; we are to fish for men as people fish for fish. We read in the Scripture of the miraculous drought of fishes, which is a picture of God's people. We are told that there are the good fish and the bad fish.

You may be familiar with the ancient Greek sign: Ichthus. It was an early Christian symbol of Jesus Christ. It is interesting that the early Christians referred to other Christians, other believers, as Ichthus, as *Pisces*, or as fishes who had been caught in the net of Christ and were now one with Him. So, even as the mythological phoenix rises out of the ashes of its own death, so also the congregation of the saints, the fishes of God, rise out of the death of the atoning sacrifice, the great day of the atonement of God.

There is also another interesting point about this that we should note: the dying goat and the fish are one. And so the Bible tells us that we are crucified with Christ; we die with Christ. The Apostle Paul said, **"I am crucified with Christ: nevertheless I live; yet not I, but Christ liveth in me" (Galatians 2:20)**. We take part and participate in that death of Christ, and out of that death we rise in newness of life with Him. This is the great picture of *Capricornus, The Sea Goat* or the Goat-fish—the fifth chapter in the great story of the Gospel in the sky.

Sagitta, The Arrow

The first decan is *Sagitta*, which simply means "The Arrow." It is the killing arrow which has been shot. It appears naked and alone. Unlike the arrow on the bow of *Sagittarius*, the archer is not seen. He who shoots it is invisible. It is a picture of the arrow which has come from the bow of God.

However, this arrow is not like the arrow of *Sagittarius* which was aimed straight at the heart of *Scorpio*, the enemy of God. But *Sagitta* is an arrow which goes forth against unrighteousness and uncleanness and wickedness, and destined for the heart of Christ.

The psalmist said prophetically in Psalm 38:2: **"For thine arrows stick fast in me."** When Jesus Christ went to the cross to die, God had bent His bow and let loose the arrows of His wrath, which pierced the very heart of Christ, bringing the lava of His wrath into the very soul of Jesus Christ.

The Apostles' Creed affirms: "He descended into hell." The real meaning of that statement is that Christ endured in body and soul upon the cross not merely the physical tortures of the crucifixion—as agonizing as those were— but the infinite anger of God against sin. Christ was made sin for us. The Lamb of God was made the "Goat" of God, the serpent upon the stick in the wilderness. And there the arrow of God's wrath was unleashed against him, sticking fast in His heart.

This is what Christ endured for us upon the cross. He endured that which sinners deserve to suffer; that which each of us deserves. This is the great central truth of the Gospel of Jesus Christ. God hath made Him to be sin for us. Christ who knew no sin was made propitiation for our sins.

In Romans chapter three, the great truth of the sinfulness of man and his inability to escape the judgment of God is set forth. But then God in His matchless mercy sets forth His Son to be a propitiation. He is to be the One against whom He will unleash His wrath "... that he might be just, and the justifier of him which believeth in Jesus" (Romans 3:26b).

Many times people simply want God to be merciful to them in the sense that they want God to relax His standards, to "lower the bar" so they can jump over it more easily. But God will not compromise. God's holy standards remain. God is of purer eyes than to look upon iniquity. He hath promised and He cannot go back upon His word. He will visit our transgressions with the rod and our iniquity with stripes. Indeed, the arrow of His wrath shall go forth and find our sin—whatever it is.

My friend, may I say to you that all of your sin will become the target of God's wrath. That arrow is coming forth in flight already unleashed from the bow of God and going forth toward your sin. It will either stick fast in your heart or it will stick in the heart of Christ. That is the great ultimate glorious story of the cross. The arrow has come to the Savior.

Aquila, The Eagle

The second decan is *Aquila, The Eagle* (the pierced, wounded and falling eagle). In all of the old zodiacs the eagle is always seen as falling. It is this one, again, who has been struck by the arrow and who is now falling.

The brightest star in this constellation is a very glorious star—*Al Tair*, a star of the first magnitude. It is familiar to all sailors who have anything to do with navigation because it is the star which is noted for the computation of longitude at sea.

Al Tair in Arabic means "The Wounding." The other stars point out the same story. *Tarared* in Hebrew means "The Wounded" or "Torn." *Al Cair* means "The Piercing." This is the eagle which is pierced by that arrow. In the tail of the eagle is *Al Okab* which means "Wounded in the Heel"—another reminiscence of the *protoevangelium*.

The eagle is a royal bird and the natural enemy of the serpent. There is an interesting phenomenon about the eagle in that it takes greater care of its young than do most other birds. In fact, it will even go to such an extent that if there is no food to be found to feed its young, the eagle has been known to tear itself with his own beak in order to feed its young with its own blood—a beautiful story and picture of Christ. The Lord is referred to a number of times in the Scripture as an eagle. We read in the Old Testament, "**. . . how I bare you on eagles' wings, and brought you unto myself**" **(Exodus 19:4)**. And again, "**As an eagle stirreth up her nest, fluttereth over her young, spreadeth abroad her wings, taketh them, beareth them on her wings: So the LORD alone did lead him**" **(Deuteronomy 32:11,12)**. Christ is that royal eagle, flying high—the one who is at the right hand of God; who thought it not robbery to be equal with God; that glorious One, the Son of God from on high. Yet, that One who humbled Himself and was pierced by the arrow of God's wrath for our sins, is seen here plummeting to the ground, the One wounded with the arrow of God's wrath.

Delphinus, The Dolphin

The final decan of this sign is *Delphinus, The Dolphin*. It is a beautiful picture of the great fish, the dolphin, vigorously leaping upward. Christ is our great Sin-bearer. But not only did He die for our sins, not only was He pierced by the arrow of God's wrath, but more than that, He plunged into the very waves of death. He says, **"All thy waves and thy billows are gone over me" (Psalm 42:7)**. And so He goes down into the waves of the deep and descends into hell. He is covered by the great stone of the tomb and His soul goes down to Hades.

We see, however, that He is not to be left there, but, rather, He rises again gloriously. As the dolphin is notorious for leaping forth out of the waves, breaking the surface and rising majestically into the air, so Christ—after His enemies thought they had once and for all done away with Him, after they had washed their hands of the whole matter and put Him aside—suddenly emerges from the waves of death as the great Conqueror of death and the grave, and rises again!

He is the principal Fish of a great multitude of fishes. Here again Jesus is identified with His people. In ancient mythology the dolphin was the most sacred and honored of fishes. Now we see that Christ has fulfilled all parts of the Gospel here. The Apostle Paul said, **"For I delivered unto you first of all that which I also received, how that Christ died for our sins according to the scriptures; And that he was buried, and that he rose again the third day according to the scriptures" (I Corinthians 15: 3,4)**. Christ is our great Conqueror.

Not only has He died and brought forth a living Church; not only has He fallen from the skies of heaven as the great Victim for our sin, enduring the arrow of God's wrath, but, also, He has risen again from the waves and billows of death to bring hope to a needy world. He is our glorious conquering Savior who fulfills all of those things which were prophesied of Him.

The Wonder of the Night Sky

How glorious it is to see that in the night sky this picture is portrayed for all of the world to see, and so we have another way, I believe, in which we can point people to that old, old story which is ever new; that story which is gloriously portrayed, not only in its figures and in its names, but even in all of the detailed names of the ancient stars. Pictures that go back beyond the recorded history of men to the very God who numbered the stars . . . who formed them . . . who sprinkled them across the sky . . . who fashioned them with His own finger . . . who gave them their names . . . and who painted for us in the galleries of the dome of the heavens, the glorious Gospel of Jesus Christ. How wondrous He is!

Prayer: We thank Thee, O Lord, for the glorious Gospel of Christ which is writ large upon the night sky and small in our Testament in our shirt pocket. We thank Thee for the same message, ever old, ever new, shining down upon the vast multitudes of this world. We thank Thee, O Christ, that we, as part of the living Church of Christ, have been brought forth as a great multitude of fishes out of the depth of the great and Final Evening Sacrifice, the great sin offering for man, even our Savior, Jesus Christ. Amen.

VI. AQUARIUS

The Water-Pourer

In the last day, that great day of the feast, Jesus
stood and cried, saying, If any man thirst, let him
come unto me, and drink. He that believeth on me,
as the scripture hath said, out of his belly shall
flow rivers of living water. (But this spake he of
the Spirit, which they that believe on him should
receive: for the Holy Ghost was not yet given;
because that Jesus was not yet glorified.)

— John 7:37-29

We come now to the subject of *Aquarius, The
Water-Bearer*, the "Pourer Forth of Water."
Notice on the planisphere, or sky chart, on the
left-hand side is a figure of a mighty man holding a great
urn upon his shoulder, from which is being poured forth
a copious stream flowing both to the east and to the west
and finally flowing into the mouth or over the body of
a fish.

You have no doubt heard the words, "It Is the Dawning
of the Age of Aquarius," from the popular song. What
does that mean? Just as the stars have moved through
the procession of the equinoxes, so we have moved from
one mansion of the zodiac to another. That procession
of the equinoxes is going in the opposite direction to that
which we have been moving in this series on the zodiac.
Interestingly, about the time Christ came into the world,
we moved into the sign of *Pisces*, which is the sign of
the fish and a symbol of the people of God. That sign
has lasted for approximately 2,000 years, after which we
will be moving into the sign of *Aquarius*, meaning a time
of peace and harmony and joy.

Aquarius means something far more than what the astrologers and others today think it means. As we have seen, *Aquarius* is the one who pours out the water upon *Piscis Australis, The Southern Fish*. Water, of course, is a great symbol of the Holy Spirit which God promised to pour out upon the earth. It is a glorious symbol of life and one of the happiest in all of the world. Jesus said, **"Come. And let him that is athirst come" (Revelation 22:17b).**

In *Aquarius* that water is being poured out upon the figure of a fish. In the sign *Capricornus* the dying goat is seen giving life to a fish emerging from its latter half. As Christ was the great sacrifice for sin and through His death the Church (or the fish) was brought into life, we now see that fish sustained in life by the risen Christ, again in *Aquarius, The Water-Bearer*, who is pouring out the water of His Holy Spirit upon the living fish (the people of God). This is a great picture of the outpouring of the Holy Spirit upon the Church of Jesus Christ.

This is a very important part of the message of Christ. It is repeated in so many ways throughout the Scripture, showing that God will pour out His Spirit like water upon a thirsty land, and that all of those who are athirst can come and drink. The Scripture ends with this fact: **"And the Spirit and the bride say, Come. And let him that is athirst come. And whosoever will, let him take the water of life freely" (Revelation 22:17).**

Those of us who receive Jesus Christ receive His Spirit into us. But as the fish lives in the medium of water, so the Christian must live in the medium of God's Spirit We are "leaky vessels" and daily must seek to be filled afresh with His Spirit. The Scripture says **"Be ye filled with the Holy Spirit."** The present tense of the Greek verb indicates: *"be ye continually getting filled with the Holy Spirit."*

Did you this day pray that God would fill you with His Spirit? Did you pray that prayer yesterday? Did you pray that prayer all through the week? We should pray every day that God would fill us with His Spirit, for without Him we can do nothing. We need to be continually getting filled with the Spirit of God. We should confess our sins; we should pray to be cleansed, and then we should pray to be filled with the Holy Spirit so that we may be empowered to serve God. If we are going to be of any use to God, it is going to be only through the power of His Spirit. The rejoicing heart is filled with the Spirit of God. When we are close to Christ and His Spirit fills us, there will be joy and gladness.

You can tell if a person is walking close with Christ by their countenance. When you see a person who is walking around downcast, with a gloomy face, you know that person is not experiencing the joy of the Holy Spirit. He does not have that happiness. It is one thing to see a fish swimming gladly through the water; it is another thing to take that same fish and throw it upon the beach!

Some Christians look more like beached fishes than fishes swimming in a gladsome pond! And without the water of God's Spirit, that is exactly what we are. We are dying without Him, gasping, and that life and joy that He would give us will not be ours. He wants to give us the joy of His presence. At His right hand there is joy forevermore. If we stay close to Him, we will receive fullness of joy from Him.

May I urge you to begin each morning of your life by praying that God will fill you with His Spirit so that He may grant you His joy and His power and that you may be used by Him for the glory of Jesus Christ. Without the infilling of that Spirit we are of no use whatsoever to God in His kingdom.

Piscis Australis, The Southern Fish

The first decan of *Aquarius, The Water-Bearer*, is *Piscis Australis, The Southern Fish*. In Greek mythology this was a representation of *Aphrodite* who was transformed or metamorphosed into a fish because she was trying to escape the horrible monster, *Typhon*. Though the truth is bedaubed with pagan mythology, I think that even now, just as they are trying to clean the dirt from the Sistine Chapel to find the original painting, so we can move away some of the incrustations of pagan myths and see the great truth that is behind the signs of the zodiac.

Even as the fish, which represents the Christian, is transformed into a new creature as he becomes part of the family of God so that he might also escape a horrible monster—not *Typhon*, but that represented as Satan—so we have been transformed by Christ into new creatures in order that we might escape the death-dealing clutches of Satan. We then live by the power of that Spirit which is constantly poured into us by Jesus Christ. We are no longer a fish being born from the dying goat of Capricornus, but are now one living gladly in the water poured forth by the risen Christ.

Pegasus, The Winged Horse

The second decan of this particular chapter as it moves on is *Pegasus*, which is above the head of *Aquarius, The Water-Bearer*. *Pegasus* in Greek means "Fountain Horse." Here is a picture of the famous winged horse flying swiftly through the heavens. This was a horse associated in mythology with glad song. It was the favorite of the muses who sent forth their gladsome songs. He is a swift, divine messenger bringing joy to all of those whom he meets.

Here we have a picture of Christ going forth with the power of His Gospel. As we have already noted, Jesus Christ is frequently portrayed in the Scripture as a figure riding upon a horse. In Revelation we find Christ mounted on a white horse. In the Old Testament, also, we have a picture of a horse going forth with the same elements: Christ going forth with the power of His Gospel, bringing great victory and with good tidings and blessings.

In *Pegasus* we see another picture of the Church, not merely as a fish receiving the fullness of the Holy Spirit, but as going forth by the power of Christ carrying the glad tidings into the world—going forth swiftly with the wings of *Pegasus, The Winged Horse*, to take the Gospel into all of the earth.

The first purpose of the Holy Spirit is to give us cleansing and joy as we rejoice in God. But, secondly, He comes to empower us for service, and that principal service is to be the messenger of the glad tidings of Christ. If we receive the power of the Spirit into our lives, we not only will live and rejoice in Christ, but we will be active in sharing the Gospel of Christ with a needy world.

As *Pegasus, The Winged Horse* flies through the heavens, so we are to fly through the earth carrying the Gospel message. I would ask you: How accurately have you fulfilled that function in this past week? Has there been one or more that you have shared that Gospel with? As Christians we should never let a week go by in which we have not talked to someone about our blessed Savior.

We have great good tidings and blessings to bring. We have "good news."

These are the meanings of the stars that are contained in that winged horse, *Pegasus*. They are messages of good tidings, of blessings. Unfortunately, for too many centuries the Church has failed to live up to its mandate to share the Gospel of Christ with others.

What is your purpose in life? What are you living for? What were you living for this past week? Did you accomplish anything that infinitely comes close to bringing eternal life and happiness to a living soul? When all of the rest of the things of this world have perished, all of those who have come to know Christ will still be living a joyful life, everlastingly, in paradise.

My friends, I hope you will consider the importance of mounting that winged steed each day and carrying the glad tidings of Christ throughout the world. What a glorious message we have and what a wonderful privilege is ours to share the Gospel with another.

If you have some timidity, obtain the training. Train yourself! Learn how to overcome your fears! Become bold for Christ! Ah, my friends, let us not let the devil silence us and cause us to be mute in the midst of a world which desperately needs to hear the message of the Gospel.

I continue to be amazed that in so called Christian America there are still tens of millions of people who have not the faintest idea of what the Gospel is.

Yes, it is a great responsibility. But more than that, it is a great opportunity; it is a wondrous privilege. I don't know of anything that brings me greater joy than to be able to share that message. Though there are vast numbers of subjects in this world that I am interested in and I have enjoyed studying, there is nothing that I would rather talk about than the wondrous love and grace of Jesus Christ. I have talked with many people about many other subjects, most of which have long been forgotten and their lives unaffected. But I have spent many an hour sharing the Gospel of Christ with people during which time their lives were transformed. They will never be the same again.

You can have that joy, too. I urge you to be part of that experience. Look up into the sky and see the winged horse, *Pegasus*, and remember the privilege that is yours to ride that white-winged horse throughout this world, bringing good tidings and blessings to those whom you meet.

Cygnus, The Swan

The last decan or part of this story of *Aquarius* is *Cygnus, The Swan*—the lordly, king-bird of the waters. It is interesting that it again ties in with the picture of the waters. *Cygnus* is one of the most beautiful of the constellations of the sky because it is the most perfectly formed cross to be found in the sky. This lovely bird, this swan, is seen here in rapid flight.

If we look at the names of the stars, there is little doubt as to what the meaning of the symbol for the swan is. The brightest star in *Cygnus* is the famous star *Deneb* which means "The Lord or Judge to Come"; the star, *Azel*, which means "He Who Goes and Returns Quickly"; and *Fafage*, which means "The Glorious Shining Forth." We have a picture of that One who died upon a cross in agony, smitten, disfigured, in whom there was no beauty when we saw Him that we should delight in Him. He is now returning as the glorious Lord, shining forth brilliantly in glory, coming as Lord and Judge of the earth, but all of the time bearing within His beautiful form that remembrance of the cross. He who comes back again is still the same One who died upon Calvary's cross. Again, the perfect picture of the glorious Gospel of Christ reaches its culmination with the return of the glorious Savior depicted in the beautiful picture of one of the loveliest of all of God's creatures: the swan.

He comes in that fashion to those of us who believe. Believers can look forward and say, **"Even so come, Lord Jesus" (Revelation 22:20b)**. Because for us He comes in all of His beauty and for us He is a delight. He is the Altogether Lovely One.

But for the unbelieving world, ah, it is an entirely different story. He comes then as an ominous One; He comes as that One who is coming to judge, destroy and condemn them because of their impenitence and their unbelief. For them the day of His coming is a day of darkness and a day of wrath. But for us, He comes as a beautiful swan! For us who are the fishes of God, who live in the water of His Spirit, He comes as the lordly King of the Waters—the beautiful Swan coming to receive his own.

My friends, when you think of the coming of Christ, does it fill you with joy and anticipation or with dread and anxiety? It all depends on whether or not you belong to Him.

Can you truly say from your heart, "Even so, Lord Jesus, quickly come"?

Prayer: We thank Thee, O God, for the beautiful story of the Gospel which is written by the pen of the Spirit in the Holy Scriptures and with a diamond pen of the finger of God in the starry heavens above. We thank Thee that the God of both is one and the same. We praise Thee, O Christ, for Thy majesty, and pray now that Thou will pour out Thy Spirit afresh upon each of us. May we receive that Spirit, even as we breathe in the air of this world so that our souls may be strengthened and filled with joy and that we may sparkle, even as the water sparkles in the dew. May we be empowered to ride forth upon the winged horse to bring the glad tidings to a parched world. For Jesus' sake. Amen.

VII. PISCES

The Fishes

The time is fulfilled, and the kingdom of God is at hand: repent ye, and believe the Gospel. Now as he walked by the sea of Galilee, he saw Simon and Andrew his brother casting a net into the sea: for they were fishers. And Jesus said unto them, Come ye after me, and I will make you to become fishers of men.

— Mark 1:15-17

As we move around the ecliptic on a planisphere, we come to the seventh major sign: *Pisces, The Fishes*. (The ecliptic is the apparent path of the sun as it moves through the sky and through the various signs of the zodiac.) In the House of *Pisces* there are two fishes, one moving toward the center of the circle toward Pole-star; the other swimming in the path of the ecliptic (the sun's path). The two fishes are united by a band securely tied around the tail portion of the body of each fish. The band is also attached to the back of the head of *Cetus, the Sea-Monster*, and *Aries, the Ram* (or Lamb) has his paw across the bands that connect the fishes.

As we have moved in our study from the direct conflict of Christ and Satan into its consequences, we have seen, for example in *Capricornus*, that the *Ram* (or Lamb) has laid down his life as a sacrifice and is dying. Yet there is emerging out of the tail of the *Ram* a very vigorous fish. The *Ram* is giving birth to a fish which we now see in *Pisces*, fully formed and swimming in the sea of the heavens.

In *Pisces* these fishes are a representation of the Church. They were indeed a symbol of Israel thousands of years ago. In fact, we use as a symbol of our church, the *Ichthus*, a picture of a fish, one of the ancient symbols of the Church. The Greek name Ichthus is an acrostic representative of Jesus' name and titles, and it is their word for "fish." The Latin name *Pisces* also means fish.

In the ancient Egyptian language this constellation was known as *Pi-Cot Orion* or *Pisces Hori*, which means "The Fish of Him Who Comes" (fishes that belong to that One who is coming, fishes that belong to Christ). It is interesting to note some of the stars in each of these fish. One of the brightest is *Al Samaca, The Upheld*. In Isaiah 41:10, God says, **"I will uphold thee with the right hand of my righteousness."** And so, as the fishes of Christ, we are upheld by the mighty hand of Christ.

The other star named from antiquity in this constellation bears the Hebrew name *Okda*, meaning "The United." We see that these two fishes are bound together. They represent the Christians of the Old Testament and the Christians of the New Testament bound together, even as we are inseparably bound to those who lived before Christ; those by whom the whole foundation for the Christian revelation was established. We are the fulfillment of them. The New Testament was intimated in the Old; the Old Testament is revealed in the New. They are bound together.

In Mark 1:17 we read that Christ said, **"Come ye after me, and I will make you to become the fishers of men."** In John 21, Jesus uses a parable in which he talks about the fisherman who lowered his net and gathered in all sorts of fishes. This Jesus likened unto the kingdom of God, which is made up of fishes contained and caught in the net of the great Fisherman. And so the Church is likened unto fishes encircled in a fisherman's net.

Perhaps we have never realized just how remarkable it is that Christ is talking to fish when He is speaking to various fishermen, such as Peter and Simon and James. He is saying to these "fish": "Follow me and I will make you fishers of men"—it is remarkable that Christ can change fish into fishers of fishes, or "fishers of men," whereby they are transformed into the fishes which make up the kingdom of God!

In Scripture the symbol of "two" is a symbol of multiplication. The Hebrew name for this constellation is *Dagim, The Fishes*, which is also related to a word for multitude. When Jacob blessed Joseph's sons he said, **"Let them grow into a multitude in the midst of the earth" (Genesis 48:16).** The margin in my Bible says "(Let them grow) as fishes do increase." It refers to the fulfillment of Genesis 1:28, **"Be fruitful and multiply."** In the New Testament we are told that the Church first added and then multiplied exceedingly. This, of course, is a picture of the great multitude of the Church which is growing.

Jesus said, **"Follow me and I will make you fishers of men."** That is a commandment followed by a promise. **"Follow me"**: a command; **"I will make you fishers of men"**: a promise. They caught something of the master-passion of the Master. There are many other similar texts in the Bible. For example, **"Believe on the Lord Jesus Christ, and thou shalt be saved" (Acts 16:31).** The same syntax, **"Believe"**: a command: **"Thou shalt be saved"**: a promise. We know, therefore, that anyone who truly, in the biblical sense of the word, *believes* (rests upon; trusts in Jesus Christ) shall be saved. Christ fulfills His promise. Conversely, we know that anyone who is not saved has never truly believed. That is so simple that every Christian would have to agree.

And yet if we try the other shoe on, it might fit a little more tightly: **"Follow me, and I will make you to become fishers of men."** It is absolutely true that if anyone follows Jesus Christ, he will become a fisher of men. It was the great passion of Christ to fish for the souls of men. Whether it was a midget up a tree, a woman by a well, a Pharisee at night—whatever the situation—Christ was constantly fishing for the souls of men. If we are going to be with Him, we are going to have to catch some of that passion.

Can you spend time with an unbeliever and not be concerned with winning his or her soul to Christ? If so, you *lack* the passion that animated the heart and soul of Jesus Christ. The disciples followed Christ; they became fishers of men. I am absolutely certain that if you could take any twelve Christians in any church in this country and have them spend three years following Jesus Christ, they would catch the passion of Christ.

But look at it the other way around. If we are not becoming fishers of men, what must be concluded? I ask you, in your own conscience, in your own mind, to answer that question. The answer is inescapable; it is ineluctable; you cannot avoid it! It must inevitably follow that if we are not becoming fishers of men, we are not following Christ. Are you a follower of Christ?

The Bands

The first decan of *Pisces* is *The Band*, (the band or bridle which connects these two fishes). We note that *Aires, The Ram* has his paw upon them. The Old Testament saints and the New Testament saints are united in Jesus Christ.

The Band makes two interesting intersections. The first is made at the back of the head of *Cetus, The Sea Monster*, a type of Satan. We must remember that we were in bondage to Satan, bound with the bands of sin. Because of the fall of mankind, the whole world was given over to the hands of the evil one. So it is, as Martin Luther said, that man supposes himself to be free when actually he is bound with a chain in his nose to Satan who turns him whithersoever he will. This is the case with each one of us. We were born in bondage to sin. The Scripture frequently refers to that bondage from which Christ has redeemed us.

The other important juncture is with the foreleg of *Aires, The Ram* (or Lamb), the next sign in our study. It is a picture of Christ with His paw placed on those *Bands* tied to the *Sea-Monster*, portraying the fact that He takes the bridle in His own hand; He redeems us from the monster Satan and sets us free. And yet we are not really free. Again, Luther said that people just suppose themselves to be free; yet there is no one in the world who is really free. We are either bound to Satan or we are bound to Christ.

One of the fishes heads toward the Pole-star and the other moves along the ecliptic. There has been some speculation about the meaning of this. It might refer to the fact that the Old Testament saints have already been taken by Christ to heaven, which according to Scripture is said to be in the extreme North; whereas the New Testament saints are continuing to follow Christ the son. **"These are they which follow the Lamb whithersoever he goeth" (Revelation 14:4).** With Christ holding onto the reins, this fish is following the Son in the ecliptic (the path of the sun through the heavens)—a picture of what the Church should be. We have been redeemed from bondage by Christ, Paul tells us in Galatians, and now we belong to Him—a picture of *The Band*.

Andromeda, The Chained Woman

The second decan of this house of *Pisces* is *Andromeda, The Chained Woman*. One of the fishes is heading right into *Andromeda* and they are connected. Here is another picture of the Church, this time not represented as a fish. By the way, in one ancient planisphere these fishes are depicted as having the face of a woman because another picture of the Church frequently used in the Scripture is that of a woman, of a bride. As the Church, we are the Bride of Jesus Christ.

Here again is another picture representing the same great truth. *Andromeda* is the figure of a beautiful woman in what appears to be a seated position, bound with chains upon her hands and feet. Her name in Greek *(Andro-meda)* means "Man-Ruler." It is interesting that though she is bound and seems to be helpless, this "helpless" woman is to be ruler of men. Though now it seems we are weak and afflicted, we are called and made by Christ to be kings and priests unto God and our Father, and we will sit in judgment upon angels as well as men. We are destined to be rulers.

The names of some of the stars in this constellation mean "the weak, the afflicted, the chained"—a picture of the present Church which is in affliction, in weakness and in chains.

In Greek mythology, *Andromeda* was the daughter of Cepheus and Cassiopeia, and the nymphs were resentful of her beauty, so they chained her to a rock near Joppa in Palestine to be devoured by the sea-monster. However, she was rescued by Perseus, who has a great sword in his hand and the head of the Medusa under his arm. He has been off in battle with the gorgons and has destroyed Medusa, a monster with serpents for hair. He has destroyed this creature of darkness and on his return from that battle with the gorgons he rescues *Andromeda* from the chains on the rock at Joppa and makes her his wife.

Pereus is obviously another portrayal of Christ, the Great Redeemer, the One who is presently engaged in a great war with the powers of darkness, the One who will succeed in utterly destroying them, the One who will destroy the head of that serpent in whatever form it comes, and will return again to free us from the weakness and the affliction and the chains of this world.

We see also in this portrayal a hatred manifested against *Andromeda*. The whole sign of *Pisces* has been an ill omen in the eyes of the world. In fact, the Assyrians and Babylonians would not even eat fish because of its connection to *Pisces*. It is a symbol of odiousness to some, just as in the eyes of the world the Church is looked upon with great disfavor.

For about 2,000 years we have been in the Age of Pisces. As the constellations move about, there is a time period in which a certain constellation gives us a particular age. In about another fifty or sixty years we shall have completed the "Age of Pisces" and shall move into the "Age of Aquarius." Through the precession of the equinoxes, because of the tilt of the earth, the stars in the zodiac are changing.

The world hates *Pisces*. They yearn for the "Age of Aquarius" to get them out of this age of the Church. So we see something of the malignant animosity of the world towards the Church of Jesus Christ. But the day will come when our Perseus, having destroyed the powers of darkness, will unchain the Church, now in weakness and in affliction and chained to the rock, waiting to be devoured. But it will not be devoured, for Christ has established it and the very gates of hell cannot prevail against it.

An interesting astronomical observation about *Andromeda* is that this constellation can sometimes be seen through binoculars—in fact, even with the naked eye. *Andromeda* (or M-31 as astronomers call it) is the closest galaxy to our own. Though everything is supposedly moving away from us, the *Andromeda* galaxy is moving toward us. It is also interesting to know that there is a galaxy composed of about 1 billion stars, approximately the same size as the Milky Way, moving directly at us at 160 miles per second! But, even at that rate, it will take a long, long time to get here because it is a million and a half light years away.

Cepheus, The Crowned King

The third and final decan in this house of *Pisces* is *Cepheus, The Crowned King*. Here we have a picture of a bearded man who wears a crown, seated upon a throne. In his uplifted hand he holds a sceptre and with his right hand he holds a portion of his robe. His right foot is placed firmly upon the Pole-star, the central point in all of the galaxies and all of the heavens. This obviously is a picture of Christ enthroned. Christ, no longer the slain Lamb (*Capricornus*, dying, giving life to the Church), but now risen and glorious and enthroned as the Great Redeemer.

Cepheus means "The (Royal) Branch or the King." In our study of *Virgo, The Virgin*, we noted in her one hand the Seed and in the other a Branch. The Branch is a name in Scripture given to Christ who is the righteous Branch who was to come. Now that Branch has been enthroned as the King.

In Egypt this constellation is known as *Per-Ku-Hor*, "This One Cometh to Rule." Here we see a picture of Christ having come to rule. The stars make it absolutely unequivocal as to who this is. The brightest star (in the right shoulder of Cepheus) is called *Al Deramin* (Arabic) which means "Coming Quickly." The second brightest star at his midriff also has an Arabian name, *Al Phirk*, "The Redeemer." At his left knee is a star named *Alrai*, meaning "He Who Bruises or Breaks."

Jesus Christ's Redeeming Work

So we see that these pictures of the fishes and of *Andromeda* are representative pictures of the Church held in bonds. But we also see that the Church has a friend ruling it, looking down from above. That One is the enthroned Christ, the great Ruler of the nations, who even now controls the destiny of the world and holds His people in His hands; who indeed has promised to uphold us, to provide for us, to protect us against all of His and our enemies and who one day will receive us unto Himself in glory.

All has come about because of the great power of our reigning, risen, and glorified Christ. How magnificent is the portrayal God has placed into the heavens for us to see on any night of the year! Praise God for His great majesty, which is seen not only in the book of Scripture but in the vault of the night sky.

Prayer: We thank Thee, O Father, for the glorious majesty of the Gospel revealed from on high. We thank Thee that the heavens declare the glory of God. We rejoice that we are in Thy hands, O Christ. We rejoice that Thou art ruling and reigning over us. Help us to be more submissive each hour of each day. Lord, make each one of us to be fishers of men that we might indeed be followers of Christ. In whose name we pray. Amen.

VIII. ARIES

The Lamb

And they sung a new song, saying, Thou art worthy to take the book, and to open the seals thereof: for thou wast slain, and has redeemed us to God by thy blood out of every kindred, and tongue, and people, and nation; and hast made us unto our God kings and priests: and we shall reign on the earth.

— Revelation 5:9,10

In our series of messages on the zodiac, we come to the subject of *Aries, The Ram or Lamb*. This second book begins and ends with an animal. It begins with a ram-like creature, *Capricornus*, which gives rise in his latter half to the birth of the fish; then there is the pouring out of the water in *Aquarius*; then *Pisces*, the two fishes; and followed by another ram-like animal, *Aries*. As one has said, they make a set of bookends to be the boundary of the Church. Thus we see, indeed, the Church begins and ends in Jesus Christ. *Capricornus* is facing toward the conflict with Satan. Though both animals are facing the same way, *Aries* is looking toward the consummation and the final victory, as found in the third book of four chapters.

A lamb is obviously a very familiar figure in the Scripture. John the Baptist began the ministry of Christ by proclaiming, **"Behold the Lamb of God, which taketh away the sin of the world" (John 1:29).** In the last book of the New Testament we read, **"Worthy is the Lamb that was slain to receive power, and riches, and wisdom, and strength, and honour, and glory, and blessing"** **(Revelation 5:12).**

There are other references in Scripture to the Lamb. There is the Lamb's Book of Life in which are written the names of God's elect. There is the wrath of the Lamb referred to in Revelation 6:16, when the Lamb becomes angry—a frightening picture depicting so mild a creature as a Lamb showing wrath. There is the Lamb who is the husband of the wife, the bride; the Bible speaks of the Church as the **"Bride of the Lamb."** There is, of course, the Lamb whose blood overcomes Satan and the saints' testimony of Him.

Let us now look at some of the names by which the constellation *Aries* has been known in various civilizations. The Hebrew name is *Taleh*, "The Lamb Sent Forth." The Greek name Krios, also means "The Lamb." In Latin it is called *Aries* (the name by which we know it) which means "The Lamb," "The Chief," "The Head." Christ is all three of those. The ancient Akkadians called this figure *Baraziggar*; *Bar* meaning "Altar," or "Sacrifice," while *Ziggar* means "Making Right." The full meaning would be "The Altar," or "The Sacrifice of Making Right." That, of course, is precisely what Christ has done. He is the great and final Evening Sacrifice of God which makes all those who believe in Him right (righteous) before God.

It is interesting to note the position of the Lamb on the planisphere. He is facing backward toward the consummation of this entire story. But one paw is placed on *The Band*, which at one end holds the two fishes of *Pisces*, and the other end is bound to the neck of *Cetus, the Sea-Monster*—one of the many pictures of Satan, the great leviathan of the Scripture.

This is a marvelous picture. If you had bands holding two large fishes on the end, and the middle of the band was tied to a huge sea-monster, it would take both hands to control it and would require every bit of your attention. But Christ has simply one paw controlling the sea-monster and He doesn't even bother to look at it! Rather, He is looking backward toward the consummation. Thus we see that with one hand He upholds the Church and also controls and restrains Satan.

The Scripture tells us that Satan is constrained by God. This is seen in the first chapter of Job, where Satan cannot do more than that which God allows him. We are told in the book of Revelation that by the power of Christ, Satan will one day be chained completely. So we see that *Aries, the Ram*, or the Lamb of God, controls both the Church and its great adversary, *Cetus, The Sea-Monster.*

There are some things about *Aries* that I think you will find fascinating. In Greek mythology there is a woman by the name of Nephele. Her name means "the Cloud." Nephele has two children, Phrixus and Helle. These children, after her death, are threatened with death by their new stepmother. The spirit of Nephele comes and warns them that they are going to be killed and that they should flee. She provides them with a large lamb with Golden Fleece. They seat themselves on the back of the lamb and take off into the air across the water, and flee to Asia Minor. Unfortunately, Helle, the girl-child, loses her hold upon the lamb's back and falls off into the sea and drowns. That water came to be known as Helle's Sea, or is better known as Hellespont.

And so it was that the antedeluvian church, before Noah's time, though faithful at one time, let go of its faith in God and drowned. The Judaistic church (the Israelite church) also turned away and mostly perished. But now, in the New Testament, we see that Phrixus, representative of the New Testament Church, continues to be borne across the sea and finally reaches the city of *Colchis*, "The

Citadel of Reconciliation," "The City of Refuge," and is saved by this lamb with the Golden Fleece. Nephele's lamb was sacrificed to Jupiter.

It is interesting that Phrixus offers the lamb himself. We are saved by the Lamb. And yet, if you stop to think about it, it was our sins which caused the death of Christ; it was our sins which placed Him upon the cross; it was our sins that brought His suffering and agony and His death. Even as Phrixus offered the lamb up to Jupiter, we have offered Him up; the Lamb dies and we are spared.

There are, of course, the well-known stories of the Golden Fleece and Jason's great adventure seeking for it. He built a ship called *Argo*, and gathered together a group of Greek heroes who became known as Argonauts. Incidentally, this has given us such names as cosmonauts and astronauts. The Argonauts set out on the *Argo*, the largest ship ever built in Greece, to find the Golden Fleece. Jason, a prince, was not able to assume his throne unless he discovered and brought back this Fleece.

Jason found that it had been hung upon an oak in a great grove guarded by a horrible monster. After discovering its location, he slew the monster with his sword and took the Golden Fleece which, when presented, gave him his claim to the throne. Even as Jason had the Golden Fleece for his cover, so the fleece of the Lamb makes a covering for us; we are clothed in the righteousness of Christ. Though distorted by pagan mythology, we have a beautiful picture of the redemption of Christ set forth here, representing the heavenly robe of Christ's righteousness—the greatest treasure of the saints of God.

That is the story of *Aries, The Lamb*—the Lamb which yielded the Golden Fleece and provides the marvelous garment of righteousness for the believer. It is the Lamb which takes us across the dangerous seas and delivers us safely to the city of refuge in Heaven; it is the Lamb which holds up the fishes of God and restrains *Cetus, The Sea-Monster*.

Cassiopeia, The Enthroned Woman

The first decan in the house of *Aries is Cassiopeia*, a woman enthroned in a chair, high and lifted up. With one hand she is arranging her robe; in the other she holds the branch of victory and is arranging her hair. The constellation *Cassiopeia* is very easily spotted in the sky. Perhaps you have looked upward and contemplated the starry heavens and have seen a beautiful "W" in the sky—the stars from which the sign *Cassiopeia* is taken. As you can see there is little relationship between the sign and the actual stars themselves.

This is a contrast to what is seen in *Andromeda*, who, like *Cassiopeia*, is a picture of the Church. *Andromeda* represents a picture of the Church in its affliction—in its bonds. *Andromeda* is in chains and left for *Cetus, The Sea-Monster* to come and devour. She is cast down. The Church today is despised by the world, is under affliction and attack, and is in danger of being destroyed and devoured by Satan.

But here we see *Cassiopeia*, (the Church), lifted up, enthroned and glorified. The decan of *Cassiopeia* means "The Enthroned Woman." In Hebrew one of the stars marking her figure is called *Shedar, The Freed*. Once bound, as Andromeda, to the rock, waiting to be devoured, *Cassiopeia* is now freed and is seated upon a throne high and lifted up. In the ancient Denderah zodiac in Egypt, her name is *Set*, which means "Set Up as a Queen." And now the Church is recognized and lifted up as the queen, ready to be married to the King of Heaven Himself.

Albumazer, an ancient authority, says this woman was anciently called "The Daughter of Splendor." The Church is now seen without spot or wrinkle—indeed a splenderous and beautiful Church, the Queen of Heaven, ready to be mated to the King. As the Bible tells us in the book of Revelation, she is ready for the marriage supper of the Lamb, which is now come. The wife has made herself ready; she is adorned for her husband. *Cassiopeia* is preparing herself. With one hand she is preparing her robes; with the other she is fixing her hair—like a typical bride preparing for the wedding feast. This is *Cassiopeia*, the wife lifted up.

Cetus, The Sea-Monster

The second figure in the house of *Aries* is *Cetus, The Sea-Monster*, which takes up more space in the sky than any other of the constellations. Of course, Satan and the world system over which he rules is so very visible and ever present, looming so large before us that sometimes we cannot even see God. And so we see *Cetus*—Satan, the Leviathan of Scripture, the great serpent, the devil—taking up a great portion of the sky. He is the monster which threatened *Andromeda* when she was chained. You will also notice that such a monster as this is the natural enemy of the fishes, which is also a picture of the Church.

Some of the stars in this constellation are interesting and their reference is clear. One of its brightest stars bears the Hebrew name *Mira*, which means "The Rebel." Satan was Lucifer, the rebel angel who rebelled against God. It is interesting to note that in most of the various constellations depicting Satan, the stars are variable—

they appear, diminish and sometimes disappear. *Mira* has disappeared for a period of four years at which time it was invisible in the sky. So Satan does his best work oftentimes when he is invisible; when people do not even believe that he is there. He is still there, however; he is still the great sea-monster seeking whom he may devour.

The brightest star, located in the nose, bears the Hebrew name, *Menkar*, "The Bound" or "Chained Enemy." Satan is the great enemy chained by Christ; the strong One. The second brightest star, found in the tail, bears a Hebrew name *Diphda*, meaning "The Overthrown." So Christ has come to this world to overthrow the kingdom and power of Satan who is thus held by *Aries* in bondage.

Perseus, The Breaker

This brings us to the final decan in this particular house of *Aries*, which is *Perseus*. In Micah 2:13, we read: **"The breaker is come up before them."** The King leads forth before them. In Hebrew the word is *Perets*, and in Greek, *Perseus*, which both mean "The Breaker," another picture of Jesus Christ.

This is very clear from the various stars found in him and the story of Christ as it is given to us in Greek mythology. *Perseus* was the son of the divine father. He was born in a most miraculous way—by a shower of gold descending upon the young woman Danae, bringing about his amazing conception. No sooner was he born, than he was put under persecution. He finally overcame that and then, as a splendid present to his father, the king, he engaged to bring to him the head of the Medusa, one of three horrible gorgons—creatures with three different heads bound together. They had defiled the temple of God. Their long hair had been turned into serpents. They were frightful creatures covered with impenetrable scales. They had tusks like boars, yellow wings, brazen hands, and were very dangerous. Their very looks had the power to turn a person into stone.

So here again is a picture of Satan. The work of Satan does turn the heart of man into a stone. But God says that He will take away our heart of stone and place within us a heart of flesh.

Perseus succeeded in this great undertaking. He beheaded the Medusa, and brought back the head, holding it by the serpents. The figure of *Perseus* on a planisphere shows him with an uplifted sword in one hand and the head of the Medusa (the gorgon) in the other hand. Here again we see a very definite bruising of the head of Satan (the *protoevangelium*).

While *Perseus* was on his way back from this brave deed, he saw the beautiful *Andromeda* chained to the rock on the coastline near Joppa waiting to be devoured by *Cetus, The Sea-Monster.* I have seen a picture showing the woman, *Andromeda*, chained to the rock and in the distance, coming up out of the sea towards her is this great sea-monster. She has something of a terrified look on her face. But in the sky can be seen *Perseus* (the great Redeemer).

The stars in *Perseus* are interesting and interpretive. In his waist is the star *Mirfak*, meaning "Who Helps." In the right shoulder is the star *Al Genib*, "The One Who Carries Away." He not only carried away the head of the Medusa, but he also carried *Andromeda* away from the rock of her enslavement into the heavenly throne, where he made her his bride.

The constellation *Medusa* itself is called *Caput Medusa*, which means the head of Medusa. In Hebrew, Medusa means the "The Trodden Underfoot." Christ is frequently represented in these pictures as treading upon the head of the Scorpion. Here, Medusa is the one who is trodden underfoot.

The brightest star in this head is *Al Ghoul*, contracted into *Algol*, meaning "The Evil Spirit." Another star in the *Medusa* head is *Rosh Satan*, which in Hebrew means "Satan's Head."

So the ancient names of the stars, indeed, reveal that truth of the revelation of God as seen in the starry heavens. Here the decan of *Perseus*, clearly depicts a picture of Christ. *Perseus* was born by a miraculous shower of gold, causing his conception; lived his whole life under persecution, but engaged, for the sake of his father the king, to take part in a great undertaking to destroy the dangerous and deadly *Medusa*, who turned men into stones. He succeeded in destroying the head, rescued the Church (Andromeda) from its slavery, broke the bonds, and set her free. He carried her up on high and married her amidst great celebration. Can this be anything else than a picture of Jesus Christ, the great Redeemer, come from heaven to redeem us, His bride?

Dear friend, I would ask you this day, as you see the wondrous consonance that exists between the story in the heavens and the story told in the Word of God, how much God has confirmed what He has said. This story is gone out into all of the earth, and the heavens do indeed declare the glory of Christ.

Prayer: Gracious Heavenly Father, we thank Thee for those twin revelations that we have: The Book of Scripture and the book of nature. We thank Thee that one confirms the other. We pray, O God, that Thou will help us to realize how true all of this is, and that our only hope to be saved from the destruction that awaits this world is found in our great Christ, the Lamb of God who taketh away the sin of the world. In His name we pray. Amen.

IX. TAURUS

The Bull

And to you who are troubled rest with us, when the Lord Jesus shall be revealed from heaven with his mighty angels, In flaming fire taking vengeance on them that know not God, and that obey not the Gospel of our Lord Jesus Christ.

— II Thessalonians 1:7,8

We now come to the final four books, the third quarternary of the zodiac. Briefly, the first four books are a picture of the suffering Savior, the coming of Christ, His battle with sin, and His suffering and death. The middle four books are bracketed by pictures of the lamb or ram, and are the story of the Church, redeemed by Christ. It is first seen as chained and desolate, and then enthroned and glorious, as in *Cassiopeia*. The final four books are the story of the consummation of all things: of the coming of Christ in judgment, of the Great Assize, of the gathering together of His own unto eternal salvation, and the fiery destruction of the wicked. It is the great culmination of the ages which is now before us.

On a planisphere, or zodiac, the ninth figure is the great constellation of *Taurus*, pictured almost at the very top (at twelve o'clock on the chart). *Taurus, The Bull*, has the same meaning in virtually every language in which it is known. It is a picture of a great beast, a bull or ox, with his head lowered and his horns pointed forward. He is untameable and irresistible. He is charging forth— rampaging, raging, head down, and bringing destruction to all who are in his way. It is a picture of the coming destruction of the wicked, as Christ comes forth in His judgment.

Taurus is only the forepart of the bull; actually it appears to grow right out of *Aries, The Lamb.* So here we see a picture of the Lamb changing into the Bull. In a previous constellation we saw *Capricornus,* half goat and half fish, giving birth to the Fish, the Church of Christ—the slain Lamb giving birth to the people of God. Here we see the Lamb now giving rise to the Christ coming in great glory and in judgment.

The chief star in *Taurus* is *Al Debaran,* located in the bull's eye, and in Arabic means "The Captain," or "The Leader," or the "Governor." And now Christ, who is the Captain of the well-fought fight, is coming forth in judgment.

As I said before, *Taurus* is located at twelve o'clock on the chart, while at the bottom at six o'clock we find the great constellation *Scorpio, The Scorpion,* a picture of Satan. We saw there Satan engaged in striking the left foot of *Orphiuchus,* the great hero above him, and being crushed with his right foot. When *Taurus* rises, then *Scorpio* sinks beneath the horizon and seems to disappear. So when Christ rises in His judgment, then Scorpio—that old serpent, the dragon, the devil—will disappear into the bottomless pit. We are told in Scripture, **"Behold, the day of the Lord cometh, cruel both with wrath and fierce anger . . . Every one that is found shall be thrust through"** (Isaiah 13:9a,15a).

Another interesting Scripture I would call to your attention is found in Isaiah 34:2 where we read: **"For the indignation of the Lord is upon all nations, and his fury upon all their armies: he hath utterly destroyed them, he hath delivered them to the slaughter."** Here is a picture of the Lord coming in judgment. In verse 7 we read: **"And the unicorns shall come down with them, and the bullocks** with the bulls; and their land shall be soaked with blood, and their dust made fat with fatness."

In reading your Bible, you have no doubt come across the term "unicorn" a number of times. As you know, the unicorn is a fabled one-horned animal. But that is not what the Hebrew Scripture says. Some translators used to translate the word in that way. But the Hebrew word is *Rheem*.

For a long time it was not known exactly what that meant, and so the translators chose the word "unicorn," and the term appears frequently in the Scripture. However, it is not really a unicorn. It has been discovered in recent times that what is really being talked about is an extinct wild ox. Though no longer alive in our day, it was around as recently as Caesar's time. In fact, Julius Caesar, in the account of his wars, describes it as being hunted in the Hercynian forests in his day.

It was a formidable creature, scarcely less than an elephant in size, but in nature, color, and form, a true ox. Remnants of this giant ox have been discovered in northern Palestine in recent times. This is not a one-horned animal, as the unicorn is generally pictured, but a very large two-horned ox. It was extremely fierce and dangerous and quite willing to attack men if ever they came into its sight. So this is a picture of what is being discussed here.

There is another interesting reference to this in Job 39:9,10, where we read: **"Will the unicorn be willing to serve thee, or abide by thy crib? Canst thou bind the unicorn with his band in the furrow, or will he harrow the valleys after thee?"** In other words, are you able to make this fiercesome creature serve you? Can you use it to herald the valleys? Can you indeed, domesticate it and use it for plowing the fields? And the answer to that is, no, you cannot. This animal is completely untameable and ferocious beyond the ability of man to restrain it. *Taurus* is this ancient, huge, wild ox or bull. It is a very fitting picture of Christ coming into judgment.

In Greek mythology, *Taurus*, this wild bull, was a form assumed by Jupiter for the purpose of carrying his loved one, the beautiful Europa, across the seas to the island of Crete. Afterward, he became angry at the injustices that had been done toward him and wrought great havoc upon his enemies. And so Christ has taken his Bride upon Him and has delivered her in safety, ultimately to heaven. He then turns in anger and judgment upon His enemies, whom He has come to destroy.

Although not a part of this particular constellation, it is interesting to note that the famous Pleiades—the Seven Sisters—one of the most beautiful little constellations in the heavens, are found riding high upon the shoulder of *Taurus*. They are a lovely picture of the Church of Christ riding upon the great bull *Taurus*, and being carried safely by him into heaven.

Orion, The Glorious One

The first decan of the three sub-points contained in this particular house of *Taurus* is *Orion*. This has always been my favorite constellation and one of the first ones that, as a child, I was able to identify. It is, indeed, a very impressive constellation. It appears in the far north as a diagonal belt of three bright stars; then two stars at the shoulders, in the legs, and in the belt across the middle. It is one of the most magnificent of all of the constellations of heaven.

Orion means "The Brilliant," "The Swift," or "He Who Cometh Forth as Light." In Hebrew the word is *Chesil*, meaning "A Strong One" or "A Hero." He is pictured as a mighty hunter. He has a club upraised in his right hand, and in his left hand he holds the skin of a lion which he has slain. There have been many who have liked to claim that this is a picture of themselves. But it is, of course, a picture of the greatest Hunter, Christ, who is the Great One.

In mythology, *Orion* was a gift of the gods to mankind— born of a woman, given by the gods, and described as the greatest hunter who ever lived—who went forth to slay all of the wild beasts. We are told, as well, that he also was the one who created the great cavern for the gods of fire.

We know that the Bible describes Satan as a lion which goeth about seeking whom he may devour. Here we see the picture of the lion's skin—the head still attached— which Orion is holding up in his left hand. We are reminded again of the *protoevangelium* (the first Gospel; the first evangel) of Genesis 3:15.

So Satan is seen as *Cetus, The Sea Monster*; as *Scorpio, The Scorpion*; as the fleeing serpent; as *Draco, The Dragon*—in the starry picture in the heavens. Christ, the protagonist, and Satan, the antagonist, are constantly portrayed in different ways in the skies above. Here again, Christ is the great conqueror of Satan.

The constellation *Orion* is mentioned three times in the Scripture: twice in Job and once in the book of Amos. It has been a famous constellation from the very beginning of time.

Orion has a bright belt or girdle about him, in which there is attached a sword. At the very top of the sword's handle is a figure of the head of a Lamb; reminding us that *Orion*, the great hunter, is also the Lamb who was slain. Now he is going forth in judgment and conquest. Keep in mind that at one time before He was the gentle Lamb, He gave Himself up to the slaughter.

One of the interesting stars in the constellation *Orion* is *Betelgeuse*, located on his right shoulder. It is a star of the first magnitude and is enormous in size. I would remind you that the diameter of the earth is almost 8,000 miles while that of our sun is about is about 865,000 miles. But the star *Betelgeuse*, is 700 million miles in diameter! The earth is about 93 million miles from the sun. This means that if the star *Betelgeuse* were positioned where the sun is, the earth in its entire orbit around the sun would be inside of the star *Betelgeuse*, since the diameter of our orbit is less then 700 million miles and the diameter of *Betelgeuse* is about 700 million miles! That great star is in the right shoulder of the arm that holds the club, which slays the lion (Satan). Indeed, we have a formidable hero in Christ.

Another famous star in this constellation is *Rigel*, found in the foot of *Orion*. It means "The Foot That Crusheth." Again, we are taken back to the picture in Genesis that the Seed of the woman is going to crush the head of the seed of the serpent, and that foot, again, is ready to crush the enemy Satan.

In *Orion's* great belt are three famous stars that are easily detected. They are called *the Three Kings*, reminiscent of the Three Kings of the Orient that tradition says came to the birth of the Son of God.

In *Orion's* shoulder is the star *Bellatrix*, which means "Quickly Coming" or "Swiftly Destroying." Christ is the One who quickly comes and swiftly destroys His enemies, particularly Satan.

Again, the picture is inescapable. In spite of all the distortion and perversion, the ancient picture given by God in the beginning still shines through all of the distortions of mythology.

Eridanus, The River

The second decan of *Taurus* is *Eridanus, The River of the Judge*. It is pictured as a fiery river that flows out of the foot of *Orion*, goes past *Cetus, The Sea-monster*, and disappears into the outer darkness. In Greek mythology it was a fiery river which threatened to burn up the world. You may ask what that has to do with the Scriptures. In the book of Daniel, we read, **"I beheld till the thrones were cast down, and the Ancient of days did sit, whose garment was white as snow, and the hair of his head like the pure wool: his throne was like the fiery flame, and his wheels as burning fire. A fiery stream issued and came forth from before him: thousand thousands ministered unto him, and ten thousand times ten thousand stood before him: the judgment was set, and the books were opened"(Daniel 7:9,10).** Here we see this fiery stream issuing forth from the Judge who comes forth to sit in judgment.

A similar picture is seen in the Psalms. **"The Lord reigneth; let the earth rejoice; let the multitude of isles be glad thereof. Clouds and darkness are round about him: righteousness and judgment are the habitation of his throne. A fire goeth before him, and burneth up his** enemies round about" (Psalm 97: 1,2,3). This is a picture of fire which comes forth from the Lord.

In the minor prophets, in the Book of Nahum, is a further reference to the same sort of judgment coming forth from the throne of God: "Who can stand before his indignation? and who can abide in the fierceness of his anger? his fury is poured out like fire, and the rocks are thrown down by him" (Nahum 1:6). Here we have a fiery stream as His fury is poured out like fire. On many of the pictures of the zodiac, this stream *Eridanus*, is shown with fire arising from it all along the way. It reaches over and touches *Cetus, The Sea-monster*, a picture of the fact that Satan is one who is destroyed; and then it descends into outer darkness, which is the picture of final judgment— the picture that is seen in the last book of the Scripture.

So here we see the darker side of the judgment—Christ coming to exercise wrath and anger upon His enemies. Indeed, it is a bleak and desolate picture: one of fierce anger and cruel wrath; one of fiery indignation and the destruction of all of the wicked. The Scripture says, "The Lord Jesus shall be revealed from heaven with his mighty angels, In flaming fire taking vengeance on them that know not God, and that obey not the Gospel of our Lord Jesus Christ" (II Thessalonians 1:7b,8)

Auriga, The Shepherd

The final decan of this house of *Taurus* is the constellation *Auriga*. On the planisphere is a picture of a man actually seated upon the Milky Way. He is *The Charioteer*, but he is also called *The Shepherd*. He holds in his right hand a band, the same band that was connected to *Pisces, The Fishes*. However, that band is no longer connected. He has a goat or a lamb in his left arm, and in his lap are two new-born baby goats. But the she-goat (the ewe, the goat or the lamb as it were) has its paws around the neck of *Auriga*. Here is a picture of the *Chief Shepherd* who shall come and gather together His own, a beautiful picture of both the adults and the children gathered together in the arms of the Shepherd.

Isaiah 40:10 describes this so beautifully: **"Behold, the Lord God will come with strong hand, and his arm shall rule for him: behold, his reward is with him, and his work before him."** Again, this is a picture of the Lord coming in judgment. **"He shall feed his flock like a shepherd: he shall gather the lambs with his arms, and carry them in his bosom, and shall gently lead those that are with young" (Isaiah 40:11).** He has His flock in His arm, as well as the young of the flock with them.

In the zodiac of Dendera (the most ancient of zodiacs) there is a slight variation on *Auriga*. In his right hand is not the bands formerly connected to the fishes; rather, there is a scepter, the upper part of which shows the head of the Lamb. The lower part of the sceptre is shaped like a cross.

This zodiac was formed even before Christ was born! And it is a beautiful picture, that in the midst of the fiery judgment and indignation . . . the outpouring of His wrath upon the wicked . . . the coming in judgment . . . the thrust through the unbelievers . . . the rising up of the wrath of the lamb in the great fury of the bull *Taurus*, the wild ox . . . the coming judgment and destruction upon unbelievers . . . we can see that Christians are safe in the bosom of the Great Shepherd, The Good Shepherd who is our Lord Jesus Christ.

How glorious is the picture and how unmistakable is the truth which God would have us to know and to heed before the coming of that Great Day.

Prayer: Father, we thank Thee for our glorious Savior; for his gentleness as a Lamb, for the fact of His power, that he is able to destroy all of His and our enemies. We thank Thee that one day He will come in great majesty and power and wrath. We pray, O God, that none of us may be outside of His grace on that day; that we may be wrapped in His arms and not standing before His horns. In Christ's name. Amen.

X. GEMINI

The Twins

And after three months we departed in a ship of Alexandria, which had wintered in the isle, whose sign was Castor and Pollux.

— Acts 28:11

On leaving the island of Melita, Paul took a ship of Alexandria whose sign, we are told, was Castor and Pollux. I am sure that many of you have read that statement in Acts 28:11, and perhaps have wondered just what it meant. It is a reference to the tenth sign that we come to in our study on the zodiac, the sign of *Gemini*.

On a planisphere, the sign of *Gemini, The Twins*, is found at about one o'clock. Along the ecliptic is seen a picture of two youthful figures seated side by side and at rest. The one on the left has a club in his hand, but even that club is at repose, leaning against his shoulder. The other figure, on the right, has a harp in one hand and a bow and arrow in the other. Here is a picture of those who have been mighty hunters or warriors, and are now seated in joyful repose. Their names in Latin were *Castor* and *Pollux*. The Greek names for them were *Apollo* and *Hercules*. *Castor* and *Pollux* are also the names of the two bright stars found in the heads of each of these two figures.

In Grecian mythology, Apollo and Hercules, the twin sons of Jupiter, were great heroes and had accomplished great exploits. They had supposedly cleared the seas of pirates. That is no doubt one of the reasons the name of the ship Paul referred to in the book of Acts was Castor and Pollux, the Latin equivalent of Apollo and Hercules. These two were very important to seamen. In fact, their names gave rise to the then vulgar form of cursing or swearing, a practice carried over today in the exclamation, "By Gemini," or the more modern "By Jiminy." That epithet came from this particular sign and from these two heroes.

The old Coptic name of this sign, *Pi Mahi*, signifies "The United," as united in fellowship or "brotherhood." *Gemini* was originally known by its Hebrew name *Thaumin, The United*. Here we have a picture of the dual nature and mission of Christ. In other pictures of the zodiac different aspects of Christ are set forth in separate figures. Here they are joined in these twin figures seated now in repose. They deal with the divine and human nature; with the mission of Christ as both Prince and Ruler, and also as Savior and Sufferer.

The figure on the right is *Apollo*, with the brightest star in *Gemini* called *Castor* which means "The Ruler" or "Judge". Here we see Christ set forth as Ruler or Judge—the Judge of all of the earth, a great part of his redemptive task. In the other figure, *Hercules*, the second brightest star *Pollux* means "The Strong One Coming to Labor or Suffer." Hercules did just that in one of his greatest accomplishments while cleaning the Augean stables of their filth. This one who came to suffer and to labor so assiduously for others is, of course, a beautiful picture of the suffering Savior who came to cleanse the filth of the world.

Another star which confirms this is located in the left foot of *Hercules*, the sufferer. It is the star of *Al Henah*, meaning "The Hurt" or "Afflicted." Again, this is a picture of the suffering of Christ as the One who was wounded in the foot by the serpent.

The next brightest star is located in the right knee of *Apollo*, and is named in Hebrew *Mebsuta*, which means *Treading Underfoot*. Once again the *protoevangelium* of Genesis 3:15.

Another star shown at the waist of the figure of *Apollo*, is Wasat (Arabic) meaning "Set". The work of these two figures is completed, and they are now sitting down, even as we are told that Christ would sit down at the right hand of the power on high. So we have here a beautiful picture of the Messiah's peaceful reign, where all of the labor and all of the suffering is accomplished. He now sits as Judge and Ruler, the God-man, the Prince and Savior of the World. It is a beautiful picture of the dual nature of Jesus Christ.

Lepus, The Enemy

When we look at the decans, the three sub-stories of this particular chapter, we see that there are some problems. We have seen that the twelve major signs have been virtually the same everywhere in all of the various countries, but there are some variations in the decans.

The first decan of *Gemini* is *Lepus*, the figure of a hare or rabbit which is under the foot or *Orion*. However, this is a relatively modern picture. Going back to a picture of the older zodiacs—such as the old Persian Planisphere—one sees that it is not a picture of a rabbit, but a picture of a serpent. Here again we have a picture of the evil one, the serpent, being trodden under the foot of *Orion*, another representation of Christ. *Orion* was the slayer of that lion that goes about **"seeking whom he may devour."** In his left hand he holds up the skin and head of a slain lion and holds a mighty club in his right hand. But now we have another picture representing Christ who is going to slay the evil one. And so with His right foot, He is about to step upon—not the hare—but the serpent.

The names of the stars make it very clear as to what is involved. In the sign of *Lepus*, the brightest star is *Arnebo*, meaning "The Enemy of Him That Cometh." Orion is that one that cometh. The brightest star in *Orion*, *Betelguesse* means "The Branch Coming." It is the huge star on Orion's right shoulder. And now we see that under his foot is the enemy of Him that cometh.

Other stars in this serpent *Lepus* tell the story very well: *Nibal, The Mad; Sugia, The Deceiver*; and *Rakis, The Bound* (in Arabic it means "Bound, as With a Chain.") The enemy of Him that cometh is called the deceiver, the mad one, the bound with a chain. In Revelation 20, John says that he saw the old serpent who was bound with a chain and cast into a pit—a perfect picture of the deceiver, that old serpent, Satan.

Canis Major, The Prince

Another problem exists with the second decan, *Canis Major*, meaning "The Greater Dog." This second constellation tells of the glorious Prince who will thus subdue the reign. In the Denderah zodiac, the oldest planisphere, which was found on the roof of a temple in Egypt, he is called *Apes*, which means "The Head." He is pictured as a hawk, the natural enemy of the serpent, coming down upon it. The name of the star is *Naz*, meaning "Caused to Come Forth," "Coming Swiftly Down." It has on its head a pestle and mortar, reminding us of the fact that Christ is going to thoroughly crush the head of the enemy, as the hawk comes down upon the serpent.

The brightest star in this constellation is *Sirius*, which in Hebrew means "Prince." It is a magnificent star which can be seen at night if stars are visible at all. A form of the word is Sar, whose root implies "To Make Oneself a Prince." The word *Sirius* represents Jesus as the Prince.

Isaiah tells us about the gift of the Son of God. **"His name shall be called Wonderful, Counsellor, The mighty God, The everlasting Father, The Prince of Peace." (Isaiah 9:6b).** Christ is frequently referred to as the Prince, the Prince of Princes; or the Prince of the kings of the earth. He is the *Sar* or *Seir*, the Prince of all the earth.

In this case, however, the star *Sirius* has been associated down through the centuries with great heat and with evil things coming upon the earth. Many centuries ago, before the precession of the equinoxes, it was associated with the coming of heat in summer. That is no longer true. But it did give rise to such things as the words of Virgil who said that *Sirius*, "With pestilential heat infects the sky." Homer spoke of it as a star "whose burning breath taints the red air with fevers, plagues, and death."

We are told in Scripture, **"And to you who are troubled rest with us, when the Lord Jesus shall be revealed from heaven with his mighty angels. In flaming fire taking vengeance on them that know not God, and that obey not the Gospel of our Lord Jesus Christ" (II Thessalonians 1:7,8).** So here is a picture of the Prince, this mighty One who is going to come with fevers, plagues and death.

It is very interesting that when the names of this constellation, *Naz (hawk)* and its major star, *Seir*, are combined, we get the words Naz-Seir. Jesus Christ is called the Naz-Seir-ene. *Naz* means "Sent" or "Caused to Come Swiftly," and *Seir* means "Prince." *Naz-Seir* means "the sent Prince," that one who is sent forth quickly; a Prince of all of the earth who is to come into the world.

Biblical scholars were at a loss to explain by what prophet or in what sacred prophecy it was said that Christ should be called a Nazarene. They had looked in vain in the Old Testament for some reference which would indicate just what that was referring to without finding it. So, though they have said (referring to the fact that He came from Nazareth) that He would be a Nazarene, there is no prophecy of that in the Old Testament. Yet the prophecy that He would be the "Sent Prince" come into the world for us has been in the sky from the beginning of creation. So here we see a picture of Christ as the Prince who comes to bring death and destruction upon unbelievers.

Canis Minor, The Redeemer

The third and final decan of this particular chapter of the zodiac is *Canis Minor, The Lesser Dog*. But again, this is a modern picture. In the ancient Denderah zodiac, it was depicted as a human figure with a hawk's head and was called *Sebak*. The brightest star in the body is *Procyon*, meaning "The Redeemer" (or redemption). So here we have in these two hawk figures confirmation of the same thing we had in *Gemini*; pictures of the two aspects of the work of Christ: The Prince—the one who comes to destroy the wicked and the one who comes bringing redemption. This is further supported by the next brightest star in this particular constellation, *Al Gomeisa*, meaning "burdened," "loaded," "bearing for others."

This is confirmed in another star in this decan called *Al Shira*, or *Al Shemeliya*, meaning the "Prince" or "Chief of the Left Hand." So we have the "Prince of the Right Hand," which is what *Canis Major* is called; and the "Prince of the Left Hand," answering to the star in *Sirius*, corresponding perfectly to the two figures in *Gemini*. Apollo represents the judge or ruler, and Hercules represents the one who comes to labor or to suffer. So, we have the Redeemer in *Canis Minor* corresponding perfectly to the two natures of Christ and the twin task of His coming into the world.

Christ Is Coming Again

We may know assuredly, as even the stars in the heavens tell us, that Christ is going to come back again. It will be a very hard time for those who are unbelievers. In fact, the star *Sirius* in *Canis Major*, because it was associated with all of the terrible calamities coming upon the earth (the searing heat, etc.) gave rise to the phrase "dog days"—days that arose from the star *Sirius*, connected with the concept of burning heat. When Christ comes back again, I assure you that for unbelievers it will be "dog days" indeed! It will be a time of flaming fire and searing heat. But believers shall be redeemed. We can rest in the fact that Christ has already won the battle. He rests at ease and reposes in glory.

As far as things down here are concerned, it is simply a time of "mopping up."

Someone once said to me that they supposed when Christ came back again that people would not recognize Him and would probably treat Him as they did at His first appearing. I replied, "My friend, you apparently haven't read what the Bible says as to the manner in which

Christ is coming. He is coming with a brightness that will eclipse the sun! Surely there will be no one who will fail to know that He has come. He will not be coming in obscurity but in greater glory, and every eye shall see Him. He will come in great power, and there is not one who will stretch forth a hand to take Him, or bind Him, or crucify Him at that time. He will be seen as He really is—in all of His majesty—the incarnate, second person of the Trinity, the Mighty God, the Savior of the world. We shall look forward to seeing the coming of our great God and Savior, Jesus Christ. All the world shall bow down and confess that Jesus Christ is the Lord to the glory of the Father."

For some, it will be the continuation of a life of adoration; for others, it will be their last act before they are cast away forever. In which group will you fall that day?

Prayer: Father, we thank Thee for the glorious picture of those great events which shall transpire one day in the future. We thank Thee that we can lift up our eyes to the brightest star in heaven and know that it is a picture of our Prince, the Prince of all of the kings of the earth. As we consider the puny individuals who lift themselves up here upon this earth and cause men to quake with fear, may we know that all of them one day will be on their faces in the dust before Him who is the King of Kings, and Prince of Princes. We thank Thee that we belong to Him and that by His great labors and suffering we have been cleansed from our sin and redeemed unto an eternal kingdom. For that we give

Thee our praise and our adoration. In Christ's great name. Amen.

XI. CANCER

The Crab

Blessed be the God and Father of our Lord Jesus Christ, which according to his abundant mercy hath begotten us again unto a lively hope by the resurrection of Jesus Christ from the dead. To an inheritance incorruptible, and undefiled, and that fadeth not away, reserved in heaven for you.

—I Peter 1:3,4

Some friends, returning from a trip to Scotland, brought me to a wall plaque which had on it the tartan, crest and motto of the Kennedy Clan. At the top of this plaque is the motto, which I found quite interesting. It contains the three French words: *Avise la Fin*, which means "Consider the End." Without having been aware of that motto in previous years it has become sort of a motto of my life.

We come now in our study on the zodiac to the eleventh chapter. We will *avise la fin*—consider the end or the completion of Messiah's work, as it relates to the redeemed.

The eleventh sign: *Cancer, The Crab*, represents "The Completion of the Redeemer's Work in Regard to His Own." This is a picture of the Church possessed and held fast by Christ. We are told by Peter that we have been redeemed **"to an inheritance incorruptible, and undefiled . . . reserved in heaven for you, Who are kept by the power of God through faith unto salvation ready to be revealed in the last time" (I Peter 1:4,5).** Here is a revelation of the keeping power of God and salvation in the heavens above.

In the midst of *Cancer, The Crab*, is one of the brightest nebulous clusters in all of the heavens called *Praesepe*, meaning "The Multitude," "The Offspring," "The Innumerable Seed." In the Old Testament, God told Abraham to look unto the heavens and if he could count the stars, so would be the number of his seed. The Church is this heavenly multitude which is kept here by God.

One of the most obvious things about a crab is the two claws by which it grasps something and holds it firmly. So here we have a picture of the Church, which is being held as a possession of Christ, taken to its heavenly home. Like the crab which lives in two elements—water and land—so the Church lives in two elements: the earth and also the heavens. Its many legs indicate multitudinous development, so the Church has multiplied exceedingly.

The Egyptian's name for this constellation is *Klaria*, meaning "The Folds," "The Resting-Places." The Syriac name is *Sartano*, which means "The One Who Holds", and is a picture of Christ who holds and keeps His own.

The word *Cancer* is related to the words, or the Noetic forms, *Khan*, which means "The Traveler's Resting Place" and *ker* or *cer*, which mean "Embraced," "Encircled." Thus *Khan-Cer* or *Cancer*, as the Romans used it, means "The Traveler's Resting Place for the Encircled" or the "Embraced." The star *Tegmine*, in the tail of the crab, means "The Sheltering" or "Hiding Place."

Another star is called in Arabic *Al Himerein*, "The Kids" or "The Lambs." then there is *Ma'alaph*, meaning "Assembled Thousands." It is a picture of the Savior's possessions held fast—the assembled thousands in the heavens above, held by the Savior and the completion of His work.

Ursa Minor, The Lesser Sheepfold

The meaning of this is made even clearer as we consider the three decans. On a planisphere *Ursa Minor* is found near the center of the ecliptic and is called today *The Little Bear*. However, this is not the ancient meaning of the constellations *Ursa Minor* and *Ursa Major*. In fact, never did a bear have such a tail as that! Actually, there is no bear in the planisphere or zodiacs of the Chaldeans, the Persians, the Egyptians, or the Indians. Rather, what we have here is a sheepfold, which is believed to be the original meaning of *Ursa Minor*.

The figure of a sheepfold probably comes from the fact that one of the brightest stars in Ursa Major is the star *Dubheh*, which means a "Herd of Animals" and is very similar to the word *Dob* or the Hebrew *Dowb*, which means "The Bear." This could be the reason the sign changed over time. But it is really referring to a little fold and a great fold. God's Church is the little flock; the gathering together of his people.

The brightest star in *Ursa Minor* is at the end of his long tail and is called in Arabic *Al-Ruccaba*. We know it as *Polaris* or *The Pole Star*, the North Star; the star in the heavens upon which the entire heavens now seem to turn. In the precession of the equinoxes, we have seen how the stars have changed over the centuries.

If we go back 6,000 years when this was first set forth, the Pole Star was not Polaris, but, rather, it was the star *Draconis*, the main star in *Draco, The Dragon*. I think it is fraught with meaning. At that time Satan had deceived Adam and Eve. He had brought them into the fall, precipitated their destruction, and now ruled over the earth. The whole world was in the hands of the evil one. So it seemed that even as they looked up into the heavens, all of the heavens rotated around the Dragon. And yet the Dragon was in for a surprise, because with the precession of the equinoxes, that has changed, and the heavens now revolve around the star *Polaris*!

By the way, the Greeks had a special word for the Pole Star. It was the *Cynosure*. Actually, the Greek word means "Dog's Tail." How they got the dog's tail on the bear I am not quite sure! But at any rate, the word cynosure has come to be a perfectly good English word. In its secondary meaning, since the cynosure is the Pole Star, it is the star to which the mariners or sailors look to for direction. And thus it became the center of attraction; the focus of all eyes. Today, we can say that a cynosure is anything upon which the attention of all the world is fixed.

I think it is interesting because here in this constellation is a picture of the body of the Church, which is actually central now in the drama of the ages. Newspaper articles concerning the rise and fall of kingdoms, concerning wars and destruction all about us, are simply the staging; the real drama has to do with the Church. What God is really concerned with in this world is what is happening in the Church. Increasingly, as that Church grows, it is becoming more and more obvious and more and more attention is being drawn to it. However, that attention is not always favorable, and people are not always happy with it. Those who are its enemies may gnash their teeth and rage, and yet it becomes increasingly a cynosure—a center of attraction.

This, of course, is even more thoroughly true of Jesus Christ, the head of the body of the Church. He is the center of the ages. H. G. Wells, who was a complete skeptic and did not believe in Christ, remarked that though he was a historian and wrote his great *Outline of History*, he found it strange that a skeptic like himself could not trace the history of this planet without realizing that more and more it came to focus in the lowly Jesus of Nazareth, who is the great Cynosure of the ages—the One to whom all eyes are increasingly turned in our world.

The next brightest star in *Ursa Minor* is *Kochab* which means "waiting Him Who Cometh." Another star is *Alpherkadain* (Arabic) which means the "Redeemed Assembly." So it is depicted as a sheepfold and not as a bear, that this little flock (this little sheepfold) is a picture of the gathering together of God's people in Heaven. This becomes increasingly obvious as we consider the next two decans of *Cancer, The Crab.*

Ursa Major, The Greater Sheepfold

The second decan is *Ursa Major*, probably the best known of all of the constellations in the sky. We don't know it as the *Great Bear*, as the Greeks called it, but we call it *The Big Dipper*. I am sure that all of us are familiar with the seven stars that make up *The Big Dipper*. They are, however, just a small part of the stars in *Ursa Major*. Like *Ursa Minor, Ursa Major* is neither a dipper nor a bear. Rather, it is the greater sheepfold, as pictured in the most ancient planispheres or zodiacs of the various nations.

In Arabic, the name of this constellation is *Al Naish*, meaning "The Assembled Together." The brightest star is *Dubheh*, "Herd" or "Fold." Another star is *Merach*, which in Hebrew means "The Flock." In Arabic it means "Purchased." The Church of Christ is His flock; they are also those whom He purchased with His own blood.

Another bright star in *Ursa Major* is *Phacda*, meaning "Visited," "Guarded," or "Numbered." We are told in the Scripture that we have been visited by the Son of God, that we have become a visited planet—visited by God incarnate; we are guarded. This is the same word found in our text where we are told that we are kept by the power of God. It means to be guarded or garrisoned. It is used in another part of the New Testament referring to a city which was guarded by soldiers and circled about. And so we are guarded or kept by God unto that salvation, ready to be revealed. We are numbered. He has counted all of His own and knows all of His elect. Their names are written in the Lamb's Book of Life.

Other stars in *Ursa Major* are *El Alcola*, "The Sheepfold"; *Cab'd al Asad*, "Multitude of the Assembled"; *El Kaphrah*, "The Protected," or in Hebrew, "The Redeemed" or "Ransomed." A more familiar star, *Callisto*, again means "The Sheepfold." So there is no doubt whatsoever, when you look at the names of the stars, they are a united and unfailing testimony. There are numerous other stars which have similar names in the two constellations of *Ursa Minor* and *Ursa Major*. Yet all point to the very same thing: this is a sheepfold containing the vast multitude of the numbered, guarded, protected, redeemed and ransomed people of God. This is the work of Christ who has gathered together His lambs into that heavenly sheepfold, that place which He has prepared for them.

Argo, The Ship

The third and final decan of *Cancer* is *Argo*. This is located outside of the ecliptic and presents the figure of a large ship. *Argo* means "The Ship." Here we have a picture of the pilgrims safe at last in harbor. In this ship, the sails are rolled up. It is not a ship in the midst of a journey, but it is a ship which has completed its journey and is now at rest in a safe harbor at home.

Here, of course, is a picture of the famous and celebrated ship of the Argonauts of Greek mythology that was mentioned before (Chapter VIII), and which apparently has some sort of historical basis. You remember the story: Jason and a great band of heroes went out on a journey in the ship *Argo* in search of the Golden Fleece. It is a picture of Christ Jesus, the Captain of the well-fought fight, the Captain of the Argonauts' ship.

The Church is pictured as a ship. The main part of a church building is called a *nave*. The ship is the ark of safety; it is the ark of Christ and Christ is the Captain. To provide that lost innocence and righteousness, Christ had to go to the city of *Colchis* and there in a garden He was hung upon a tree guarded by a serpent. Jason (Christ) alone was able to destroy the serpent and recover that righteousness, this Golden Fleece, which now had been transformed as having come from the sheep that was killed. It is a picture of Christ, the Lamb of God, who gave his life to provide a covering for man's lost righteousness.

The *Argo* and all of its heroes have endured the many trials and sufferings and dangers and now at last the ship has been brought safely home to a harbor of rest.

The word *Argo* comes from roots meaning "The Company of Travelers." The brightest star in *Argo* is *Canopus*, meaning "The Possession of Him Who Cometh." Another star, *Sephina*, means "The Multitude." *Tureis* means "The Possession"—once again, a picture of the possessions of Christ.

There is an interesting thing about the ship of the Argonauts. On the prow is featured the head of a lion. On all ships the head of whatever creature they featured faced forward, but on *Argo* the head is facing into the nave of the ship, looking down upon those who inhabited and sailed in that ship.

Christ, of course, is the great Lion of the tribe of Judah. He is the One who is protecting and watching over His own. So here we have a picture of the ship of the Church, of the nave, arriving at last after its dangerous journey. Having secured the Golden Fleece to cover its nakedness—produced by the slain Lamb which gave its life for their covering—now, at last, with sails rolled up, it is at peace and at ease in the harbor and haven above.

Indeed, *avise la fin*—consider the end; the completion of Messiah's work. As far as we who are believers are concerned, this is the glorious task. We who are kept by the power of God are gathered at last into the sheepfold prepared by Christ. We are brought at the end into that peaceful harbor and haven of rest, by the glory and power of our great Redeemer and Captain, Jesus Christ.

This is a beautiful picture and I trust that henceforth, whenever you see a picture of the sign of *Cancer*, you will have an altogether different conception of the meaning. I trust you will remember that you are held in the hand of Him from whom no one can take you; that there is reserved for you a place in heaven; that you are kept by the very power of God.

Prayer: Father, we thank Thee for the glory of the Gospel of Jesus Christ. We thank Thee for the accomplished and finished work of our Savior, that we will at last join our voices with the vast multitudes coming out of every tongue and nation and tribe upon this earth, and cry in exaltation: "Our Jesus hath brought us all the way to glory!" In His name. Amen.

XII. LEO
The Lion

**And I beheld, and, lo, in the midst of the throne
and of the four beasts, and in the midst of the elders,
stood a Lamb as it had been slain, having seven
horns and seven eyes, which are the seven Spirits
of God sent forth into all the earth.**

—Revelation 5:6

We come now to the twelfth and final chapter of
our study on the Zodiac: *Leo, The Lion*. I trust
that as we have made this adventure around the
great ecliptic of the heaven, that your faith and wonder
at the glory of God and His amazing revelation have been
strengthened—both in the book of Scripture and in the
book of nature, His special revelation and His general
revelation.

The name of this constellation, *Leo, The Lion*, means
virtually the same, whether you look at it in Arabic,
Hebrew, Coptic, or Syriac. It means "He That Rends, That
Tears Asunder." The lion is a majestic, kingly, and noble
creature. It is king of beasts in the jungle and is spiritually
represented by the King of Kings.

The lion is a familiar figure in Scripture. In fact, the
word "lion" appears some 98 times. If you add "lions,"
"lion's," and "lionesses," they total about 150. In Genesis
49, Jacob gave his blessing to Judah, his son. He said
that Judah would be a lion. David, the great son of Judah,
was a man of war and went forth to conquer. And so the
greater Son of David is Jesus Christ, who is described
in Scripture as **"the lion of the Tribe of Judah; the Root
of David."**

In Revelation 5:5 John was told: **"Weep not: behold, the Lion of the tribe of Judah, the Root of David, hath prevailed to open the book"**—this book which contained the mystic blessings of God, which seemed to have been forfeited by the sin of man forever and which is sealed up and forever kept from man. And there is none who is able to release the seven seals and restore to man the lost blessing. But it came, and there was only one who could prevail. That one was a lion. John was called to look upon this Lion, and when he looked, behold, he saw a Lamb as it had been slain.

So we see the connection between the Lamb of God which taketh away the sin of the world, and the Lion of the Tribe of Judah. At His first coming into this world, Jesus, as the Lamb of God, came meekly and humbly to lay down His life, to shed His blood for the sins of the world. As the Lion of God, He is seen as the representation of His second coming, where He shall come in great power and glory.

This is clearly seen in many places in Scripture. In the Old Testament book of Hosea, we see God represented as a lion: **"Therefore I will be unto them as a lion: as a leopard by the way will I observe them: I will meet them as a bear that is bereaved of her whelps, and will rend the caul of their heart, and there will I devour them like a lion: the wild beast shall tear them"** (Hosea 13:7,8). So God says that like a lion he will tear them and rend their hearts.

In the Psalms, again we see God representing himself in this same way: **"Now consider this, ye that forget God, lest I tear you in pieces, and there be none to deliver"** (Psalm 50:22). The constellation of *Leo, The Lion* means "He That Tears Asunder." And God represents Himself in that way. When He becomes manifest and incarnate in this world, it is precisely as the Lion of the Tribe of Judah.

The stars in this particular constellation make the meaning even clearer. The chief star, situated in the lion's breast, whence its mighty paws proceed, bears the name of *Regal*, which means "The Treading Underfoot." That is precisely what the feet of the lion can do. In fact, Joseph Seiss, author of *The Gospel in the Stars*, tells us that the forepaw of the lion can exert the same force as dropping a twenty-five pound hammer. With one blow of its paw it can break the backbone of an ox or crush the skull of a horse. With one blow its claws can cut four inches in depth on another beast. No wonder man is ill-equipped to fight with a lion! Indeed, it is an awesome and terrifying representation of God when He is stirred up to wrath.

In this last of the constellations, the feet of the lion are about to land on the head or neck of the serpent. In the Psalms we read: **"Thou shalt tread upon the lion and adder: the young lion and the dragon shalt thou trample under feet" (Psalm 91:13).** Here we see that the Lion is about to trample that old serpent underfoot .

Some of the other stars in this particular constellation are *Denebola*, which means "The Judge," "The Lord Who Cometh Quickly"; *Zosma*, meaning "The Shining Forth," the "Epiphany" (or manifestation, as when Christ shall come again); *Minchir al Asad*, meaning in Arabic "The Punishing" or "Tearing of Him Who Lays Waste"; *Al Defera*, meaning "The Putting Down of the Enemy." Here, indeed, is a vivid picture of the wrath of the Lamb; the coming forth of Christ in final judgment and victory over His foes.

In the sign of *Cancer, The Crab*, and all of its decans, the saints are finally held securely by Christ and are brought at last into the heavenly arch, into safe harbor, and into home at the end. Christ has finally securely brought His own unto Himself. But before the end there is the destruction of His enemies. In this final sign of *Leo* it is equally clear and incontestable that this is a picture of the destruction of the wicked.

Hydra, The Serpent

The first decan of *Leo* is the sign of *Hydra*, which is a great serpent. On a planisphere it is seen insidiously stretching itself along the right third of the heavenly skies, outside of the ecliptic, with the head beneath the feet of the lion. This, of course, reminds us again of the *protoevangelium*, that first presentation of the Gospel. These star pictures are again simply an exposition that Christ will destroy the head of the serpent, the seed of the serpent. Here we find that being brought into completion.

We see that Lucifer (meaning "light-bearer"), the angel of light and the most glorious of God's creations, was cast down and became Satan, the Prince of Darkness, because of the sin and pride. Indeed, that is a tragic change when you consider the meaning of his original name, the "Bearer of Light."

Christ, we are told in Scripture, came into this world in order to destroy the works of Satan, and to that end all of His acts and all of His administrations are aimed. In this final picture, Satan is about to fall into the cluthes (the claws) of the Lion and to be destroyed. Here Christ's arch enemy is about to be trampled beneath the feet of *Leo, The Lion.*

The great Serpent was first seen at the center of the ecliptic. One of the stars in *Draco, The Dragon* was originally the Pole Star located at the very center. And that is where Satan was after he had insinuated his way into the Garden of Eden and had cast his slime across the path of the history of man, deceiving and destroying mankind, and bringing all of the world into subjection to his vile will. He was at the center of all things; the Prince of this earth, the Prince of the power of the air.

But now we see that Satan is cast out. He is outside the great circle of the ecliptic. He is about to be finally destroyed by Christ and cast into utter and final darkness. We are told in Revelation 20 that Satan is finally bound with a great chain and cast into a bottomless pit, and from thence into everlasting fire.

There are many myths about *Hydra*. In Greek mythology, the great monster *Hydra* dwelt in the Lernaean lake—a picture of the corruption and vilenes of this world. It was said to be a hundred—headed monster (from which the term "hydra-headed" monster is derived). Every time somebody would cut off one of Hydra's heads, two others would appear, making it impossible to be destroyed in that way.

This is a picture of the evil and wickedness in this world. These heads of *Hydra* could only be destroyed by fire. One of Herakles' (in Roman, Hercules) great tasks was to destroy the hydra-headed monster, which he did by cutting off the heads, and then applied a red hot iron to sear the wounds to prevent them from multiplying again. Herakles, of course, represented another picture of Christ.

The name *Hydra* means "He Is the Abhorred." The brightest star in this constellation is located in the neck of the monster and is called *Al Phard*, meaning "The Separated," "The Excluded," "The Put Out of the Way." John tells us that he (the Devil) shall be bound with a great chain and cast into a bottomless pit. Another star in the constellation is *Minchir al Sugia*, meaning "Tearing To Shreds of the Deceiver."

Satan is known as that old deceiver, and this battle with mankind is fought with deception. He uses the weapon of deception; he deceives the minds of men; he is a liar from the beginning; he deceived Eve with a lie: he deceives people with the lie that they will find their greatest joy apart from God. Perhaps Satan's most successful lie of all times is deceiving millions of people down through the ages into believing that joy and fulfillment and satisfaction are found in the things of the world—apart from God. This lie has been incredibly successful.

Another lie of Satan's is that we can *earn* our own acceptance before God; by our own strivings we can make ourselves acceptable in the sight of God. One of the first lies passed on to the descendants of Adam and Eve is seen in their own children, as Cain tried by the fruits of his own labors to earn his acceptance with God. Countless millions of people have been deceived by that lie. What lie is Satan using on you? The Bible tells us that we shall know the truth and the truth shall make us free.

Crater, The Cup

The second decan in this final sign is *Crater, The Cup*. It is called "The Cup of Wrath." In Revelation 14:10 we read: **"The same shall drink of the wine of the wrath of God, which is poured out without mixture into the cup** of his indignation; and he shall be tormented with fire and brimstone in the presence of the holy angels, and in the presence of the Lamb: And the smoke of their torment ascendeth up for ever and ever: and they have no rest day nor night, who worship the beast and his image, and whosoever receiveth the mark of his name."

In Psalm 11:6 we read, "Upon the wicked he shall rain snares, fire and brimstone, and an horrible tempest: this shall be the portion of their cup." A cup which contains a "fire and brimstone, and an horrible tempest." Indeed, a horrible cup to contemplate. In Psalm 75:8 we read more about that cup: "For in the hand of the Lord there is a cup, and the wine is red; it is full of mixture; and he poureth out of the same: but the dregs thereof, all the wicked of the earth shall wring them out, and drink them."

It is interesting, I think, that this cup is fixed right on the back of the Serpent. As a matter of fact, the two stars which make up the base of the cup are also a part of the Serpent, so that the cup is affixed to *Hydra, The Serpent.* We are reminded that it was through the serpent that the curse originally came into the world. Accursed is the world for his sake, the Lord told us back in Genesis. Because of Satan, this curse has come into this world. This curse, which has so plagued the world over the centuries, is now to be poured out upon Satan and upon all of his followers.

Corvus, The Raven

Finally, we come to the third and last decan of *Leo,* the final figure in the great gallery and portraiture of the heavens, known as *Corvus, The Raven.* On a planisphere the Raven is also shown on the back of the Serpent. All three of the decans of *Leo* are connected, and are outside the ecliptic of the sun. Here is a picture of life in outer darkness, cast away forever.

In Proverbs 30:17 we are told **"The eye that mocketh at his father, and despiseth to obey his mother, the ravens of the valley shall pick it out."** Remember how David said to Goliath, **"I will smite thee, and take thine head from thee; and I will give the carcases of the host of the Philistines this day unto the fowl of the air, and to the wild beasts of the earth" (I Samuel 17:46).** This is a picture of the final destruction of the wicked.

In Revelation 19 we see the final picture of these dark fowls of the air coming in their final destruction. Also seen here is the great and final battle of the Lord, when Christ comes forth on a white horse with the name upon His vesture: King of Kings, and Lord of Lords. In Revelation 19: 17,18 we read: **"And I saw an angel standing in the sun; and he cried with a loud voice, saying to all the fowls that fly in the midst of heaven, Come and gather yourselves together unto the supper of the great God; That ye may eat the flesh of kings, and the flesh of captains, and the flesh of mighty men, and the flesh of horses, and of them that sit on them, and the flesh of all men, both free and bond, both small and great."** We see the beast and the kings of the earth and their armies gathered together. Here is the great picture of the battle of Armageddon.

We go on to read of the final great act in the history of the world in the last verse of chapter 19: **"And the remnant were slain with the sword of him [Christ] that sat upon the horse, which sword proceeded out of his mouth: and all the fowls were filled with their flesh" (Revelation 19:21).** So we come to the final word in the final battle of this earth, and it ends with the fowls being filled with the flesh of those that followed the beast and believed his lie.

And so we come now, also, to the very end of this great circle of teachings from the heavens, to *Corvus, The Raven*, and the fowls of the air ascending upon the Serpent, the leader of the forces of evil. The name of this constellation in Arabic is *Minchir al Gorab*, which means "The Raven's Piercing or Tearing To Pieces." The brightest star, located in the eye of this ill-omened bird is called *Al Chiba*, which comes from the Hebrew and means "The Curse Inflicted."

Is there any doubt as to what the meaning of this final chapter is for unbelievers? It is the final destruction of the ungodly, the unbelieving, by the coming of Christ in all of His mighty glory—the end of the serpent and of his crew.

Prayer: Father, we thank Thee for the Bible written in pen and ink. We thank Thee for the story of salvation, which is written in the diamond-studded pen of the starry skies. We pray that from each we may draw our inspiration and faith and say, "O Lord, our God, how great Thou art." Through Jesus Christ our Lord. Amen.

XIII. WHAT ABOUT ASTROLOGY AND HOROSCOPES

Thou art wearied in the multitude of thy counsels. Let now the astrologers, the stargazers, the monthly prognosticators, stand up, and save thee from these things that shall come upon thee.

—Isaiah 47:13

As our study of the zodiac has shown, from the beginning of recorded time, man has demonstrated an almost insatiable urge to know the future—to pierce beyond the veil of tomorrow and know what lies ahead in this life and the next. All manner of divination or efforts to foretell the future have been tried. One that has been perhaps the most venerable and long-standing, and now is coming back to popularity, is astrology. Having been banned from the universities three hundred years ago by the rise of modern astronomy, it is again on the rise.

I have related some of the tremendous amount of historical evidence showing that what is now known as astrology is a pagan corruption of an original revelation given by God and drawn by His hand. The *Mazzaroth*— the signs of the zodiac—are brought forth each night by God. They were sprinkled by His hand across the sky as He garnished the heavens and created the figures which we now know as the figures of the zodiac. In the book of Job we read: **"Canst thou bring forth Mazzaroth [meaning the constellations of the zodiac] in his season?" (Job 38: 32a).** They tell a glorious tale of redemption, a pictorial representation of the first promise of the Gospel, the *protoevangelium*.

I would like to repeat that the Bible very explicitly condemns astrology in all forms and those who look unto astrologers as well. We are to have nothing to do with this pagan corruption. We are to see not divine gods or influences that can sway our lives, but rather the story of a Savior who can affect and transform our lives.

So many people are taken up with astrology today. One wag, when asked what sign he was born under, said, "The best, I remember it said Maternity Ward."

You might respond, when asked that question, "I was born under the sign of the cross." That is a good sign to be born under.

But perhaps something which might elicit a more interesting conversation is a response a young lady told me that she uses. She responds in this way: "I have a slight problem when you ask me what sign I was born under, because I was born twice!"

This usually elicits the question: "Oh! What do you mean?" That answer gives you a good entry into spiritual matters, and if you can't be off and running with that, you don't know much about sharing the Gospel.

Let's take a brief look at astrology and horoscopes from the Christian perspective. The word "horoscope" comes from two Greek words which mean to observe the hour or the time. How accurate are they? I have looked at the horoscope for this week and I wonder just how accurate it is for you today. Let us, for example, look at a horoscope which appeared in the paper. Were you born under the sign of *Pisces*? For those of you who may be less enlightened in the occult arts, let me inform you that means you were born between February 20 and March 20. Let us see how your horoscope worked out for yesterday. It says that "you must express your ideas with conviction if you want to impress others."

It will surprise you how horoscopes fall in line. If that one does not apply to you, there is always the horoscope in another paper, and if that doesn't do it there are still approximately 9,998 others in the United States alone, plus 15,000 more outside of this country that you can turn to for a professional reading of your horoscope!

People are credulous today; IBM computers shoot out over 30,000 personalized horoscopes every month to shoppers in department store malls. And if that doesn't satisfy their need, there is always the twenty-four hour a day service you can call long distance and get up-to-the-minute predictions by computerized astrological services. Another company has astrological services located on the campuses of two thousand universities in this country. You see what our students are learning?

Some of the errors of astrology are rather famous and many people may know about them. For example, what did Hitler learn from astrology? He was one of the first popularizers of the modern resurgence of astrology. He had five full-time, paid astrologers on his staff, helping him run the Third Reich. Now it is interesting what happened.

He had, at first, some rather remarkable successes as he moved his armies into battle, withdrew them, or withheld them according to the dictates of the stars. Many of these predictions are nothing more than trite platitudes, such as, "work hard and you'll succeed" and "early to bed and early to rise makes a man healthy, wealthy and wise"—which are true for most people most of the time, regardless of when you were born or what day it is. Nevertheless, it is also true that astrology has had some rather remarkable successes. And so did Hitler for a while; but he ended in disaster and was burned up in the flames. Perhaps there is something that we may learn from what he learned in the ultimate deception of those who follow these things.

Another famous boo-boo of the astrologers was when Apollo 8 was orbiting the moon. It was a most notable time. The astrologer said that Jupiter and Uranus were in conjunction for the first time in fourteen years and this flight would be, no doubt, accompanied by grave perils and by terrible catastrophes. But Apollo 8 went up and Apollo 8 came down, and nothing disastrous happened.

And then, on February 3, 1962, five major planets were in conjunction, lined up straight through the sun and the earth, and simultaneously the sun was eclipsed by the moon. Astrologers issued dire warnings about floods and earthquakes and disasters, and some even warned of the end of the world. But February 3, 1962, came and went and nothing unusual happened. Another error occurred when Jeane Dixon prophesied that half of California was going to fall off into the ocean! Many people sold their homes and moved out of California!

One secular physician stated that astrology makes people dependent. It weakens their character; it deprives them of their ability to make intelligent and rational choices. They become addicted to this, and the lives of many people have been utterly destroyed. For example, there was the man who went to an astrologer and was told that he would marry young, but that his first wife would not be the wife of his dreams or the wife who would bring him happiness, and that he would marry a second time and this woman would bring him lifetime happiness.

He married almost immediately after that, but he told someone on his wedding day that this was not the woman of his dreams nor the woman who would bring him happiness—that he had to marry her in order to find the second one. She was a lovely girl and made a delightful wife, but he was so impressed by the fatalistic claim of this astrologer that a year and a half later he deserted her, divorced her and found another wife—the woman of his dreams. A short time later she became a fanatical cultist and drove him out of his mind. Finally he had to leave her, too, deceived by an astrologer, with his life almost destroyed.

Then there was a woman who came, distraughtly, into the police station and told the sergeant that she had just shot and killed her son because her astrologer had told her that her son, who was having mental problems, would never overcome them. She was so distraught at the idea that her child would have such a miserable life, that she took a gun and shot him in the head. All this, because of the guidance of an astrologer.

We are told by astrologers that we are passing out of the age of *Pisces*, which was an age focused upon the death of Christ, and that we are moving into the age of *Aquarius, The Water Bearer*, an age of peace—the golden age. Carroll Righter tells us it began in 1904. Well, did it? They said they were going to be the golden years, but they turned out to be the bloody years and included World War I, World War II, Korea and Vietnam. They said the age would be a time of peace and pleasure and joy; when before people were focused on the death of Christ, now they would turn away from Him.

What does the Bible say about this? It says a great deal. It talks about, in numerous places, the matter of divination, of divining the future, of trying to ascertain what will happen. The Hebrew word for a diviner means a *divider*, one who divides things. On the basis of the way in which they are divided, he foretells the future. And so these people base their hopes upon chance, and anything that pertains to chance will do.

For example, a battle and the throw of dice are both equally unknown as to their outcome. But the dice can be tested, and it is assumed that the result of the dice will be the same as the result of the battle, and so one throws the dice and ascertains what the future shall be. It doesn't matter whether it is the dice, whether it is the shuffling of cards, and the dealing thereof (such as Taro cards), or the flight of birds, or the dregs of some drink, the reading of tea leaves, or even the very ancient art of hepatoscopy, any matter of chance will suffice.

Hepatoscopy, according to one authority on the subject, is the art from which astrology arose. It is an examination or observance of the liver of sheep. A person brought a sheep as a sacrifice, and the sheep was slain. The liver was taken out and examined, and it was assumed that the liver of the sacrificial animal was a microcosm of the universe. (We find that we have a brass model of a sheep's liver dating back to the third century B.C. in Rome, and even a clay model dating all the way back to the time of Hammurbi in Babylon.) The edge of the liver is divided into sixteen sections, and they are given names of deities which occupy those sixteen sections of heaven, as the Babylonians conceived it at that time. The position which the liver fell into supposedly indicted how the gods in the outer world were going to respond to the person who brought in this sheep.

The authority on Hepatoscopy points out that the Babylonian ideograph or word for planet is a combination of the two Babylonian words "dead sheep." When the planets were finally discovered, when they finally were ascertained to be something different from the fixed stars, they were named after the liver of a sheep which was offered. The idea was that in the stars we had some indication of how the gods were going to favor us.

At first they divided the zodiac into four divisions—north, east, south and west—and then later into twelve. Then they added more so they could get more of a variety of horoscopes by giving free constellations or stars to each one of the twelve houses of the zodiac.

They say that the light from these stars comes and affects people at the time of their birth. Shakespeare refers to Romeo and Juliet as star-crossed lovers who, because of the stars under which they were born, were destined to have a tragic romance, and there was nothing they could do about it. This is fatalism at its worst.

The two things many people do not realize is that, first of all, the Babylonians who invented this and the Romans who practiced it were under the Ptolemaic concept of the universe, which said that the whole universe circled around the earth, and which we now know, from Copernicus, is not true. Furthermore, they thought that there were only five planets, but since seven was the perfect number, they included the moon and the sun and called them planets too—which we also know is not true. So the whole Ptolemaic concept is wrong.

This concept is even more completely invalidated by the fact (which is not recognized by astronomers) that there is what is known as the precession of the equinoxes, meaning that the earth is tilting on its equinox (and the sun also), so that it is moving some fifty seconds through the circle per year. This means that from the time this whole system was established by the Babylonians until today, it is almost *two months off*; and the constellations supposed to inhabit these various houses aren't even there anymore.

And so, if the light from these stars is affecting us, the system is completely wrong. This doesn't bother the devotee to astrology because, after all, he is not concerned with scientific answers anyway. But the Bible makes it clear that this is related to heathen worship. It is related to the worship of the heavenly host, which the Bible condemns.

In Amos 5:26 it says this: **"Ye have borne the tabernacle of your Moloch and Chiun [the Hebrew word for Saturn] your images, the star of your god . . ."** Saturn was the best known of the planets in the Old Testament, and it was the star of the god Moloch. It is interesting to note that this god was the most vicious of the gods of the Old Testament. In the hands of this brass image a great fire was created. Children were put in the red hot hands and were burned to death as an offering. God was saying to the Israelites, **"You are bearing the tabernacle of your king Moloch and you are worshiping his star, Saturn."**

Over and over again worship of the heavenly host is condemned. **"Take ye therefore good heed unto yourselves . . . lest thou lift up thine eyes unto heaven, and when thou seest the sun, and the moon, and the stars, even all the host of heaven, shouldest be driven to worship them, and serve them" (Deuteronomy 4:15,19).** And those who did such things in the Old Testament were commanded to be stoned unto death. In Isaiah 65:11,12 (NIV), it says, **"You who forsake the Lord . . . who spread a table for Fortune and fill bowls of mixed wine for Destiny, I will destine you for the sword, and you will all bend down for the slaughter."** Well, what is fortune and what is destiny? Jupiter and Venus are the greater and lesser good fortunes of the astrologer. The Scripture says that you forsake Jehovah as your guide if you look for these.

We see in the Scripture that Lucifer (Satan) is a shining star. He is the light bearer; he is the symbol of the planet Venus, a planet of good fortune according to the astrologers. Satan doesn't care whether you become overtly, explicitly and confessedly a worshipper of Satan or whether you turn from God subtly and even unknowingly to receive direction and guidance for your life from the host of heaven and from Satan as the prince of the powers of the air. Here is the shining star, and in the darkness of the night, people find guidance and direction in the host of heaven; they seek their good from them and do not even know they have turned from the living God and are following the directions of Satan.

Hitler found out all too late, too tragically, as many others have. That is why, I am sure, that when that woman shot her son, it was not the first time she had read an astrological table. She had no doubt read them hundreds and hundreds of times before. And do you know what? Many times they were accurate.

So Saturn lures us to follow this and lures us to believe his lies, and finally, when we are convinced, he leads us astray and away from the living God. The Bible says that the Son of Righteousness, Jesus Christ, is to rise and shine upon us and to dispel the darkness of the night. When Christ comes and the light of His glory shines into our hearts and minds, we will see the folly of following after these things and seeking our guidance from them. We cannot combine the two. God condemns it out—rightly.

A young lady said to me, "Do you know what my sign is?"

I said, "No, what is it?"

She said, "My sign is the sign of the Cross." In Hoc Signo—(in this sign conquer), in the sign of the cross of Jesus Christ. You may have been born under the sign of *Cancer*, but you are born again under the sign of the cross. If you are guided by the stars of the heaven, you are guided by the evil one, unknowingly, no doubt. But if you are guided by the sign of the cross and you seek His face in His Word, you have the direction and guidance of God, who said that His Word is a lamp unto our feet and a light unto our path, the One that will never fail us. We can *know!*

- *We can know* that we have been redeemed and we can know the future.

- *We can know* that we shall be with Him forever.

- *We can know* for certain that we are going to go to heaven because Jesus Christ has taken our sins upon Him, because He has paid the debt for our sin.

- *We can know* that our sin is forgiven.

- *We can know* that we are on our way to paradise.

- *We can know* that God has said that he will never leave us or forsake us.

- *We can know* that he will turn all things together for good to those that are His own, if we seek Him, the true and living God, and if the sun of His love, the Son of righteousness, arises and causes the light of the glory of His Gospel to shine upon our hearts.

From which source do you seek guidance for your life? And, therefore, whom are you really following?

Prayer: Lord, may we not be deceived by the subtleties of Satan who can make himself an angel of light, and who lets out much line and offers much bait that he may deceive men and ensnare them and drag them down into hell. Let us turn from the hosts of heaven and turn unto the Lord of heaven and earth; and may the light of the glory of His grace shine upon our hearts. May we trust in His Cross and rejoice in that sign, now and forevermore. And to Him be all praise and honor everlastingly. Amen.

XIV. SUMMARY

The Serpent Destroyed

In the beginning of our study of the zodiac we noted that all of this was an unfolding of the truth that was hidden, like the bud of a flower, in the *protoevangelium* of Genesis 3:15: **"And I will put enmity between thee and the woman, and between thy seed and her seed; it shall bruise thy head, and thou shalt bruise his heel."**

We have seen this conflict presented to us over and over again in our study. For example, in the beginning of the story, *Virgo, The Virgin,* is seen bringing forth the Seed, who is going to be engaged in the salvation and justification of man, represented in *Libra, The Scales.* Then immediately we see the conflict beginning and the price to be paid as *Scorpio* (the first picture of this serpent—the devil) stings the mighty man *Orphiuchus* in the heel but in turn is crushed beneath the right heel of this mighty man. Again, we see the devil portrayed as a serpent *(Serpens)*, struggling and wriggling in the hands of *Orphiuchus*, and reaching up to try to take the crown away from God, just as we are told in the Old Testament that Satan would attempt to do.

We then see Satan represented in *Cetus, The Sea Monster*, who was seeking after *Pisces, The Fishes*, representative of the people of God, as he *(Cetus)* attempts to destroy them. Again, we see Satan destroyed by *Orion* (Christ), who holds in his hand the dead carcass of the lion (Satan), who goes about seeking whom he may devour.

And then Satan is represented by the head of the gorgon Medusa, having serpents for hair and which is slain by

Perseus. Finally, he is represented here by *Hydra, The Great Serpent*, who covers so much of the sky.

But now in this final chapter, the serpent is triply destroyed by the feet of the lion, by the outpouring of the cup of wrath, and by the devouring fowls of the air, depicted in *Corvus, The Raven*.

But in all of the six pictures of the serpent we notice the conflict between Satan and Christ. In *Scorpio*, the first one, he is being crushed by *Orphiuchus*, and *Sagittarius* is aiming his arrow at his heart. The serpent, seeking after the crown, is being held securely by *Orphiuchus*, the strong and mighty hero that is Christ. *Cetus, The Sea Monster*, is held under the foot of *Aries, The Lamb*, and is tied with the bands that are held by the lamb. The lion, who was to go about seeking whom he may devour, has been killed by *Orion*; the gorgon Medusa has been slain by *Perseus*; and *Hydra* is finally to be consumed once and for all by the lion. So in every case we see this constant conflict between the serpent and Christ, and in every case we see that Christ is more than conqueror.

Worthy Is the Lamb

So the glorious picture does have an ending. It is not like the pagan view of time, which is an endless circle going round forever and ever and ever. We do not come back to the version bringing forth another Christ to start the cycle all over again. We finally come to the climax, as the Scripture tells us, when one day an angel will reach forth his hand and place it on the wheel of time. He will stop that great wheel and declare with a loud voice, "Time shall be no more." God will drop the final curtain upon the drama of the ages and this world will come to a great climactic and final end. God's drama of redemption will be completed. And we will be singing then, **"Worthy is the Lamb that was slain to receive power, and riches, and wisdom, and strength, and honor, and glory, and dominion forever and ever and ever."**

Why Preach on the Zodiac

In conclusion, let me say that the reasons for my dealing with the zodiac at all are:

- To show how this study overthrows the higher critical view on the origin of Christianity. (Some French critics gathered together all of the ancient myths and said that Christianity was simply a repetition of those myths. They did not realize that those myths were simply the corruption of an earlier revelation given by God in the very beginning of mankind.)

- To show the true origin of pagan mythologies as a distortion of God's original revelation.

- To show how the Gospel has been preached and proclaimed to the whole earth.

- To show the divine origin of the Scriptures which proclaim the very same message written by the hand of God in the stars.

- To show that astrology is but a satanic distortion of an original revelation from God; that it is a corruption, a deception on the part of the great deceiver, the great counterfeiter, Satan.

- To preach the old, old story of the glad tidings with a new voice that resounds from the very vault of heaven so that in some way I may catch the attention and then the hearts of some hearers whose ears may have become dull to chapter and verse.

- And last, but of great importance, to magnify Jesus Christ, whose virgin birth ... whose glorious life ... whose atoning death ... are all writ large with a diamond pen by the very hand of God in the glittering panorama of the night sky.

How wondrous is the age-old story God has painted for us. In the days and months and years to come, I hope you will look up into the wonders of that sky and see coruscating above you the myriad of stars which the Bible tells us God has placed there with His own hand—that He has garnished the heavens with His own fingers and placed these constellations there. He has given them their names; He brings forth the Mazzaroth in their season.

He has done all of this that the glory of Jesus Christ and the wonderful drama of his redemption might go forth into all of the earth. And as we look up at that sky, may our hearts be filled with wonder and praise.

XV. SIGNIFICANCE OF THE TWELVE SIGNS FROM A CHRISTIAN PERSPECTIVE

VIRGO—THE SEED OF THE WOMAN

Speaks of Christ as the incarnate Son of God who will be 100 percent divine and 100 percent human (Genesis 3:15).

LIBRA—THE REQUIRED PRICE PAID

Relates to Christ as the Redeemer who paid the full price of sin (Isaiah 53).

SCORPIO—THE MORTAL CONFLICT

Set forth Christ as wounded for our transgressions, and the bruising of Christ's heel as necessary for victory over Satan (II Corinthians 5:21).

SAGITTARIUS—THE FINAL TRIUMPH

Portrays Christ, the God-man, as the victor over sin and Satan (I John 3:8).

CAPRICORNUS—LIFE OUT OF DEATH

Illustrates that through Christ's death for our sins we are made spiritually alive (John 12:24).

AQUARIUS—BLESSING OUT OF VICTORY

Speaks of the joy of God's Spirit poured out on His people as the fruit of Jesus' victory (John 7:37).

PISCES—DELIVERANCE OUT OF BONDAGE

Foretells of God's deliverance of people of all nations from the slavery of sin into the glorious light of His love through the preaching of the Gospel (Matthew 4:18,19).

ARIES—GLORY OUT OF HUMILIATION

Illustrates how, although Christ was humbled and slain as "the lamb of God," He has been raised from the dead and made the Ruler of all creation (Revelation 5:12).

TAURUS—HIS GLORIOUS COMING

Foretells that Christ will come in judgment like a rampaging bull upon the sinful world (Isaiah 34:2-8).

GEMINI—HIS UNION WITH HIS BRIDE

Speaks of Christ's fellowship with His people in His eternal kingdom (I Thessalonians 4:17).

CANCER—HIS POSSESSIONS HELD SECURE

Assures us of God's fulfillment of His promise that He will have a great kingdom filled with a multitude of people from every race, tribe, and nation (Genesis 22:17).

LEO—HIS ENEMIES DESTROYED

Prophetically assures us that Jesus Christ shall be victorious over sin, the world, and Satan (Revelation 5:5).

XVI. BOOKS HELPFUL IN RESEARCHING THE SUBJECT OF THE ZODIAC

Banks, William D. *The Heavens Declare*, Kirkwood Missouri: Impact Books, 1985.

Bullinger, E.W. *Witness of the Stars*. Grand Rapids, Michigan: Kregal, 1893, 1967.

Carr-Harris, Bertha. *The Hieroglyphics of the Heavens*, Toronto: Armac Press, 1933.

Fleming, Kenneth C. *God's Voice in the Stars: Zodiac Signs and Bible Truth*. Neptune, New Jersey, 1981.

Morris, Henery M. *Many Infallible Proofs*. San Diego: Creation-Life Publishers, 1974.

Rolleston, Frances. *Mazzaroth or The Constellations*. Keswick, England, 1863.

Seiss, Joseph A. *The Gospel in the Stars*. Castel Press, 1884, Grand Rapids, Michigan: Kregal, 1979.

Spenser, Duane E. *Mazzaroth*. San Antonio: Word of Grace, 1972.

NOTES

NOTES

NOTES

NOTES